OUT IN THE OPEN

Jonathan Harvey comes from Liverpool and now lives in London. His plays include: *The Cherry Blossom Tree* (Liverpool Playhouse Studio, 1987); *Mohair* (Royal Court Theatre Upstairs, 1988); *Tripping and Falling* (Glasshouse Theatre Company, Manchester, 1989); *Catch* (Spring Street Theatre, Hull, 1990); *Lady Snogs The Blues* (Lincoln Arts Festival, 1991); *Wildfire* (Royal Court Theatre Upstairs, 1992); *Beautiful Thing* (Bush Theatre, London, 1993 and Donmar Warehouse, London/Duke of York's Theatre, London, 1994), winner of the John Whiting Award 1994; *Babies* (Royal National Theatre Studio/Royal Court Theatre, 1994), winner of the George Devine Award 1993 and *Evening Standard*'s Most Promising Playwright Award, 1994; *Boom Bang-A-Bang* (Bush Theatre, 1995); *Rupert Street Lonely Hearts Club* (English Touring Theatre/Contact Theatre Company, 1995), winner, *Manchester Evening News* Best New Play Award, 1996; *Swan Song* (Pleasance, Edinburgh/Hampstead Theatre, London, 1997); *Guiding Star* (Everyman Theatre, Liverpool/Royal National Theatre, 1998); *Hushabye Mountain* (English Touring Theatre, 1999). Television and film work includes: *West End Girls* (Carlton), *Beautiful Thing* (Channel Four/Island World Productions), *Gimme, Gimme, Gimme* (Tiger Aspect/BBC2), *Dinner At Tiffany's*, an episode of *Murder Most Horrid* (BBC2).

OUT IN THE OPEN

Jonathan Harvey

Methuen Drama

Methuen Drama

2 4 6 8 10 9 7 5 3 1

Copyright © 2001 by Jonathan Harvey

The right of Jonathan Harvey to be identified as the author of this work
has been asserted by him in accordance with the Copyright, Designs
and Patents Act, 1988

First published in Great Britain in 2001
by Methuen Publishing Limited

A CIP catalogue record for this book is available from the British Library

ISBN 0 413 76250 5

Typeset by SX Composing DTP, Rayleigh, Essex

Out in the Open

Out in the Open was first performed at the Hampstead Theatre, London, on 15 March 2001. The cast was as follows:

Tony	Mark Bonnar
Iggy	James McAvoy
Mary	Linda Bassett
Kevin	Sean Gallagher
Monica	Michele Austin
Rose	Vilma Hollingbery

Directed by Kathy Burke
Designed by Michael Taylor
Lighting by Chris Davey
Sound by Dean Whiskens

Characters

Tony, *Scottish, thirty-three. His partner Frankie died six months ago.*
Iggy, *Mancunian, twenty-one, looks like a rent boy.*
Mary, *Londoner, fifty-five. Never shuts up, nervous. Frankie's mum.*
Kevin, *Londoner, thirty-three. An alcoholic. Frankie's best mate from school.*
Monica, *black, thirty, a bit overweight. A waitress who wants to act.*
Rose, *a friend of Mary's. In her sixties, a big drinker.*

Setting

The play is set over one long weekend in the back garden of Tony's ground floor flat in Dalston, London, summer 2000. There is a set of French windows into the living room of the flat and an entry up the side of the house that leads to the street. The garden wouldn't look out of place on an episode of *Ground Force*. There is a step up from the house, and the raised area is covered in tasteful decking. Night lights hang on the wall in jars. There is a water feature and a barbecue. Nice benches and a table fitted into the design, matching the decking. Plants in pots. Fairy lights. The cordless phone seems to live on the garden table.

Act One

Scene One

Friday night.

The lights come up on **Tony**'s *garden, night-time. A hot summer's evening. The light is on in the living room and fairy lights light the decking, along with nightlights and candles.* **Tony** *stands by the house.* **Iggy** *is seated.* **Tony** *has a bottle of lager.* **Iggy** *is drinking something fizzy from a glass.*

Tony   My begonias haven't come out.

Iggy   Yeah?

Tony   Yeah. Sod's law, eh?

Iggy *takes a swig of his drink.*

Tony   They should be this gorgeous cerise colour. But all I've got is shoots. The guy in the shop promised me they'd be fabulous. Erm. Sorry. I always revert to stereotype when I'm a bit on edge.

Iggy   Why are you on edge?

Tony   I'm fine. So. D'you like the garden?

Iggy   Yeah. Sit here.

Tony   OK.

He sits next to **Iggy**.

Hello.

Iggy   Why are you on edge?

Tony   I'm not.

Iggy   You said you were.

Tony   I'm full of shite.

Iggy   You are single, aren't you?

Tony   What? Well, that's just it you see. My boyfriend's inside. He's got a terrible temper on him. (*Beat.*) Yeah. I'm single.

Iggy   But someone else lives here?

Tony   Only my lodger. He's out. I think. Maybe I should go and check.

Iggy   Have you always been single?

Tony   No. No, I was with someone for seven years. Look at the size of your hands. Hold them up.

They hold a hand up against hand to compare sizes. They rub hands.

Iggy   You've never done a hard day's graft in your life, have you? So soft.

Tony   Cheeky bastard. At least I've not got an old man's hands.

Iggy   What happened?

Tony   He died.

Iggy   Shit, I'm sorry. Was it recent?

Tony   Six months ago. Is that recent? It feels recent.

Iggy   Shit. What was his name?

Tony   Frankie.

Iggy *wretches.*

Iggy   Sorry.

Tony   You all right?

Iggy   It's this. (*Indicates the glass.*) It's minging. What is it again?

Tony   Dioralyte. Try this. (*Passes him the beer.*) So do you have a bloke?

Iggy   No one'll have me.

Tony   I don't believe that for one second.

Iggy   I just split up with someone.

Tony   Long-term?

Iggy *shrugs.*

Iggy   D'you work as a gardener?

Tony *shakes his head.*

Tony   Who did the ditching?

Iggy   Him.

Tony   He's a fool. Did you never show him your eyes? It's Frankie's birthday today.

Iggy   How old would he have been?

Tony   Thirty-three. Ancient.

Iggy   It's not ancient.

Tony   How old are you? Don't tell me you're still at school.

Iggy   Fuck off, twenty-one. I'm at college me. Photography.

Tony   The camera never lies.

Iggy   How old are you?

Tony   Forty-five next birthday. I know I don't look it.

Iggy   Really? God. You only look about thirty-eight.

Tony   I'm thirty-three.

Iggy   Good job I go for older men then, innit?

Tony   If you're looking for a father figure I draw the line at you calling me dad.

Iggy   As if.

Tony   Was he old?

Iggy   I don't wanna talk about him.

Pause.

Tony   So what brings you to London?

Iggy   Felt like it.

Tony   I remember the days when I did things just cos I felt like it.

Iggy   Wanted to get him out me system.

Tony   But why did you end up in that pub? I'da thought a pretty boy like you would've been heading up to Soho.

Iggy   I was. Then I got the shits. D'you go there often?

Tony   Is that you chatting me up?

Iggy   No. It's a question.

Tony   Dunno. Couple of times a week. We used to go together. Had our own quiz team. The Dalston Darlings. I only go now when the boredom sets in. When I'm sick of fiddling with my decking. This isn't a garden by the way, it's therapy.

Iggy   D'you miss him?

Tony   Of course I do. He was my best pal.

Iggy   I'm a nosy twat, aren't I?

Tony   You're a very beautiful twat, I'll give you that.

Iggy   I think you're pissed, mate.

Tony   I used to be beautiful, believe it or not.

Iggy   What went wrong?

Tony *pours some lager on his hand and flicks it at* **Iggy**, *playfully.*

Tony   Is Iggy short for Ignatius?

Iggy   Sadly.

Tony   Good Catholic lad, eh?

Iggy   Oh yeah.

Tony   Would it be possible to see you naked at any point this evening?

Iggy   What if I tell you to fuck off?

Tony   You won't tell me to fuck off. I bought you a pint. You came home with me. I tried to cure your shits.

Iggy   Yeah and you made me fucking sick.

Tony   You have a duty to let me see your naked form, it's only fair!

Iggy   You're fucking barmy, you.

Tony   Down here . . . if you agree to go back with someone. That's it. There has to be nakedness.

Iggy   Nudity.

Tony   That too. I'm sorry. It's a while since I've done this.

Iggy   Have you not had anyone else since him?

Tony   To be honest I've not fancied it. 'Til now.

Iggy   And what if I said I don't do out on a first date?

Tony   I'd call you a liar.

Iggy   I don't feel well.

Tony   That's fine. As long as I can just sit here and look at you for a bit longer.

Iggy   Sounds to me like you're getting over him.

Tony   You're over him too. His ashes are buried right under you.

Iggy   Fuck off!

Tony *laughs.*

Iggy   Freak.

Tony   Sorry.

Iggy   What was the funeral like?

Tony *gets up angrily.*

Tony   Oh, it was great. A real laugh. What d'you wanna know about my boyfriend's funeral for? Turn you on, does it? All this talk about death? Bit of a necrophiliac, are you?

Iggy   I'm only trying to be nice.

Tony   It rained. OK? There was a lot of crying. Particularly from me. Almost wailing at one point. Nicole Farhi and snot, not an attractive combination. Kevin, my lodger, he was at school with Frankie, he did a reading. Another friend Monica sang 'Here Comes the Flood' by Bette Midler. His mother was inconsolable, she still is. We had the wake back at his favourite restaurant in Smithfields, and later on we all went to a club.

He starts to cry.

This isn't right. This is so not right.

Iggy *steps over and takes* **Tony***'s face in his hands and slowly kisses him. They snog for a while.* **Iggy** *pulls away tenderly.*

Iggy   Sorry. Couldn't help meself.

Tony   I haven't been with anyone your age since . . . well, since I was your age.

Iggy *gets up and walks to the French windows. He stands there and looks at* **Tony***, trying to look all sexy.*

Tony   Where d'you think you're going?

Iggy   Where's the bedroom?

Tony   Tired?

Iggy   No.

Tony   You can't possibly fancy me.

Iggy   I asked you a question.

Tony   I'm not very good at describing.

Iggy   Well, perhaps you better show me.

Tony   OK.

Iggy *sniffs and looks down at his trainers.*

Iggy   I think I've trod in something.

Tony   Oh, that'll be next door's cat, sorry. Slip your trainers off.

Iggy *slips his trainers off.*

Iggy   I've not had a bath today.

Tony   Is that supposed to turn me on?

Iggy   D'you have a shower?

Tony   Into the hall, second door on your right.

Iggy   I thought you were crap at describing.

Tony   I'm afraid there's no lock on the door.

Iggy   Pervert.

Iggy *goes inside, leaving his trainers outside.* **Tony** *rests his head in his hands. He sits there for a while, lost in thought. He gets up and blows the candles out, then switches the fairy lights off. He looks up to the heavens and smiles. He calls out to the sky.*

Tony   You bastard!

Blackout.

Scene Two

Saturday morning.

The next morning. **Tony** *comes out in his dressing gown with a dustpan and brush and a mop. He goes to brush away the cat shit on the decking. The French windows are open and the telly is on. It's a warm sunny day.* **Iggy***'s trainers sit on the floor outside the French windows where he left them last night.*

Tony (*shouts to neighbours*)   You should sew that cat's arse up! How would you like it if I came over and crapped on your grass?

He sweeps the shit into the dustpan and throws it over the fence.
Mary *bounds through the gate with three plastic bags. Two contain watermelons, one contains shopping.*

Mary   Oh no! He hasn't done it again, has he?

Tony   Mary?!

Mary   Hello, darling. Oh and all over your lovely decking look. What you done to your hair?

Tony   I'm just up.

As she speaks he goes about mopping the decking.

Mary   You ever tried Maurice on the high street? He's good. No, he is good, darling, trained in Paris. But don't, whatever you do, get saddled with Kisha-Louise. What she's doing in a salon of that calibre I'll never know.

Tony   Did you want a cuppa?

Mary   Ooh no, darling. I only popped in to give you these. (*She empties two large watermelons onto the table.*) I seen 'em up Ridley Road, darling. They got your name on 'em.

Tony   Where?

Mary   It's a saying, darling.

Tony   It's a joke, Mary. Sit down, I'll stick the kettle on.

Mary   No, I can't stop. Honestly, darling. I'm looking in on me lady with the leg, darling, and I'm late as it is.

Tony   Well, if you're sure.

Mary   Mind you, I've come all this way. And I don't suppose I'll get a bus straight away, bastards.

Tony   Tea?

Mary (*grabs his arm and pulls him close*)   What's that funny one you give me last time darling?

Tony   Sage.

Mary   Have you got any left? Cos I'll have normal if I'm putting you out.

Tony   You're not. It's a glorious day, isn't it?

Tony *exits with the watermelons.* **Mary** *gets a joint out of her handbag and lights up.*

Mary   That's the only word for it. (*Spying* **Iggy**'s *trainers.*) Oh, Tony. You got yourself a new pair o'pumps, darling? Ooh, they're nice and fancy. Here, you'll never guess what. Bloody optician says I need a new pair o'glasses. I can stick with what I got for reading, but I need another set for watching the bloody telly. 'Blimey!' I said. 'I'll have more glasses than Stringfellows.'

Kevin *comes in, pissed, just woken up.*

Mary   Oh Kevin. No work today?

Kevin   No.

He picks up a bottle of Hooch off the garden table.

Mary   How's your lovely old nana keeping?

Kevin   She's got shingles.

Mary   What, round her trunk?

Kevin   Yeah.

Mary   Cor, that's nasty. Send her me best, won't you?

Kevin   If you want.

He exits. **Mary** *starts mopping the decking.* **Tony** *comes back out.* **Kevin** *sits watching the telly indoors during the following.*

Tony   Mary, I can do that.

Mary   Oh, shut up. Want some o'this? (*Offers him the joint.*) Go on darling. I hate smoking it on me own.

Tony   No, I'm trying not to.

Mary   Oh, me too. But see, it's me rheumatoid arthritis, darling. I'm not supposed to carry anything heavier than a bag o'sugar.

Tony   Well, what were you doing buying two fucking watermelons?

He goes back inside. **Mary** *calls the next speech through to him.*

Mary   I had this terrible dream last night, Tony. Horrible it was. I'm up John Lewis in Brent Cross and I'm in the basement, when the woman next to me in the queue sets fire to herself. And it starts to spread. So I leg it up all the escalators to get to the roof.

Tony *comes out with a bowl of hot soapy water and a scrubbing brush. He goes about cleaning the dirt off* **Iggy**'s *trainers.*

Mary   Then I has to jump off the roof, on to this big stack o'sofas. And all the firemen there was off *London's Burning*. But I can't stand *London's Burning*. What d'you reckon that means? They were really nice actually. Specially the Greek one. I was about to have a little cuddle and that with him only I woke up.

Tony   Who's the lady with the leg?

Mary   Three doors down, moved in last month. I only get her a few bits, she's ever so grateful. Had a ramp built up to her porch. I said to her, I said, 'Council didn't waste no time with you, darling. Shame they weren't like that with my wonky bath.' Eighteen months it took to level it out. I had a deep end and a shallow end. You taken your pills today, darling?

Tony   Aye. Why's she had a ramp built? That's pretty postmodern, isn't it?

Mary   She can't manage steps, darling. She's got one o'them funny wheelchairs what look like them golfing car things. Sort o'thing Magnum drove. She's got one o' them for going the post office only I won't let her. Cos she drinks, darling. She thinks I don't know. But I found fifteen miniature vodka bottles up her entry. She's a dangerous driver. She's had three crashes since she moved in.

Tony   She goes on the road in it?

Mary   Well, she's not supposed to, obviously. But she's so fucking paralytic she can't see where she's going. And we've got that school round the back of us. I worry for them kiddies. Anyway she won't be going out in it again. I hid the keys. (*Pats her pocket.*)

Tony   She sounds like a laugh.

Mary   Oh, she's lovely, Tony. No she is lovely. Showers her home help with toffees, coasters, you name it. Just, you know, bit of an alky. And I mean, between you and me, she smells a bit. Home help says it's got a name.

Tony   Oh well, if she's in a wheelchair maybe it's difficult for her. You know, like . . . washing and stuff.

Mary   No apparently she's always had it. Persistent Fish Odour Syndrome. Tries to cover it up with Charlie, bless her. But fuck me she is rank. Nice though. Lost a son in the Falklands, so we usually have a natter about that side o'things. Husband used to hit her.

Tony   That's terrible! And her in a wheelchair.

Mary   Reading between the lines . . . he put her in it. Oh, I shouldn't say things like that. He ain't here to defend himself.

Tony   Dead?

Mary   Birmingham. Well, the outskirts.

Tony   I'll check the kettle.

Mary   Yeah, hurry up, darling. I'm on a schedule. And make sure you wash your hands!

Tony *exits.*

Mary   Can I use your phone darling? Give her a quick tinkle? (*Dials number.*) She'll be sat by that window. She relies on me Tony. I'm her lifeline. (*On phone.*) Hello, darling, it's me. Now I'm up Dalston so don't get yourself in a tizzy, I know you. Now, I got everything on the list but they didn't have that scent you wanted so I got an alternative. (*Gets it out.*) Passion, darling. What will they think of next? Your nice home help been round? Ah, has she? Has her sister had that baby yet?

Pause.

Harelip's nothing these days, Myra. See ya!

Tony *comes in and gives her a cup of tea.* **Mary** *puts the phone down.*

Tony   You're not stopping long, are you? I'm supposed to be in work in an hour.

Mary   I went up the grave yesterday. Nice flowers. You're ever so thoughtful, darling.

Tony   I've not been up for a few weeks.

Mary   Ain't you? Well, who put the flowers there?

Tony   I don't know.

Mary   But yesterday was the thirteenth, darling. You said . . .

Tony   I got tied up at work.

Mary   But it was his birthday, darling.

Tony   I know it was his fucking birthday, Mary. What did you want me to do? Go up there and bake a cake? I got tied up at work. I might go later.

Mary   This phone's filthy.

She gives it a wipe with her cloth.

Tony   I was going to go.

Mary   What got you tied up at work then darling? I hope they ain't working you too hard. When I met your manager at Frankie's send-off I thought she had a touch of the Adolfs about her. Right bossy cow.

Tony   One of my team's got shingles. So I'm covering for him.

Mary   Ooh, that's a debilitating disease, shingles. Kevin's nan's got that, ain't she. Cor. There's a lot of it about, Tony. You wanna make sure you don't get it. It's like being punched in the side with a crowbar, you know.

Kevin *comes out in sunglasses with his Hooch.*

Mary   'Ere, Kevin. One of his team's got shingles an' all.

Kevin   Great. What's a doppelgänger?

Mary   Type o'German sausage, innit?

Kevin   Is it?

Tony   No. It's a looky-likey. Why?

Mary   Is it? Oh.

Kevin   They just said it on the telly. Didn't know what it was.

Mary   What you been doing with this phone, Kevin? It's filthy. Look at the colour of that!

Kevin   I've been making dirty phone calls, Mare.

Mary   You didn't call me, did you? Years back? I got an heavy breather the day Princess Diane died. Some people have got no respect for the dead.

Kevin   Yes, it was me.

Mary   I blew a whistle down the phone. Frankie said I should've asked him out. Cheeky little git. You been up Frankie's grave, Kev?

Kevin   No.

Mary   Only there was some nice red roses up there yesterday. Thought it mighta been you.

Kevin   Well, it weren't.

Mary   Oh well. Probably Monica.

Kevin   Monica's in Greece.

Mary   The musical?

Kevin   The country.

Tony   Lucky cow.

Mary   Oh, cos she had that audition.

Tony   That was for *Mamma Mia*.

Mary   She'd be good in that. She's got a lovely voice.

Kevin *grunts.*

Mary   Kevin!

Tony   What I wouldn't give to be lying on a beach just now.

Mary   She sung lovely at Frankie's send-off. D'you know who she reminds me of? She's like a black . . .

Kevin   Bella Emberg?

Mary   Jane MacDonald. Now she can sell a tune.

Tony   I think she's back today.

Mary   That's what Monica wants to do. She wants to get on one o'them docusoaps. She'd be lovely in one o'them. She'd be lovely in a lot of things.

Tony   Frankie always fancied Mykonos.

Mary   Did he?

Tony   We were always planning to go together.

Mary   He never told me.

Tony   I wanted to go with Monica, do it for Frankie. But I couldn't get the time off work.

Mary   D'you know what this tea tastes like?

Kevin   Piss?

Mary   Bovril. I haven't had that for years. I used to give it Frankie if there was a nip in the air. He couldn't get enough of it. I thought he was addicted at one point. Nearly took him up Dr French. Well, if it wasn't Monica, who was it?

Kevin   Didn't they leave a card or nothing?

Mary   No. Looks lovely though, Kevin. You should get yourself up there. All them flowers. Call yourself a friend. And I took tiger tulips. I'm so pleased we went for that marble in the end.

Kevin   I don't need to go to no cemetery to remember him.

Mary   There's a new grave two doors up. Looks lovely. They went for the photograph on the headstone. Lovely looking woman. Got a look of Gloria Hunniford about her. I do think it's nice to put a face to the name.

Tony   Mary . . .

Mary   Don't shout me down darling.

Kevin   That's so tacky!

Mary   I still say . . .

Tony   Mary!

Pause.

Kevin   Why's it called doppelgänger?

Tony   I dunno. I think it's a German word.

Kevin   God, couldn't we even think up one of our own?

Tony   We did. Looky-likey.

Mary   Give it a little clean, you know. Found this fabulous marble cleaner up Windsor last week. Had an excursion. Saw the castle then went to a garden centre. Lovely stuff for your garden there. And I found this marble cleaner. I thought, 'I'm having some o'that!' Brought the grave up lovely.

Tony   What were you doing up Windsor?

Mary   Keeping my mate Rose company, wan' I? She's always going on day trips with her drop-in centre and she likes me to go with her cos most of 'em are doped up to the eyeballs on antipsychotics. She's going Hastings for a fortnight next week. B&B, evening meal and round-the-clock care. It's marvellous. It's Blair's Britain.

Kevin   I think I'm getting a cold sore.

Mary   Oh. That'll be your herpes back with a vengeance. Oh, I better be off. Use those watermelons wisely.

She stands.

D'you know? The menopause don't half make you dizzy. (*Kisses* **Tony**. *To* **Kevin**.) I'm not kissing you, you dirty bugger. You taken your pills today, Tony?

Tony   Yes.

Mary   Well don't forget. Oh. (*To* **Kevin**.) Will you be seeing Dodgy Rog this week?

Kevin   Maybe.

Mary   That stuff's fantastic. Purely medicinal.

Kevin   I'll get some more.

Mary   OK. I get paid Friday so I'll sort you out then.

Kevin   Whatever.

Mary   And don't work too hard up that shop, Tony!

Mary *exits.* **Kevin** *is still standing in the doorway.*

Tony   You look like shite. What time did you roll in?

Kevin   You ain't my nan.

Tony   I'll tell you when. Five o'clock. Who did you bring back?

Kevin   I don't have to answer to you.

Tony   Can you remember?

Kevin *thinks.*

Kevin   I met him up the heath.

Tony   Is that supposed to be funny?

Kevin   Oh, I'm sorry. No, I am, I'm really sorry. How you feeling today?

Tony   Kev I don't mind you having fellas back but for fuck's sake keep the noise down next time, eh? I'm going back to bed.

Kevin   I thought you was goina work?

Tony   I lied. OK?

Tony *picks up the trainers and goes in.* **Kevin** *looks up at the sky.*

Blackout.

Scene Three

Saturday afternoon.

A few hours later. **Monica** *sits in a deckchair, rolling a cigarette. She wears a friendship bangle round her wrist. On the table sit two presents in brown paper bags from a gift shop. The trainers have disappeared.*

Monica   I've decided.

Kevin (*off*)   What?

Monica   I'm gonna be a performance poet.

Kevin *comes out with a cup of tea and a bottle of Hooch.*

Kevin   Why?

Monica   I wrote some poetry in Mykonos.

Kevin   Is this mine?

Monica   Yeah it's a present. I think you'll like it actually.

Kevin (*unwrapping present*)   Is it a gay Mecca?

He has unwrapped a cup.

Monica   It's a cup. It's got a picture of me on it.

Kevin   You narcissistic bitch. Was there millions of queens there?

Monica   Yeah. Well, a few. There were quite a lot in the gay bars. Met a nice couple from Stanmore. They were cool. Had some really mellow chats with them. They bought me this on the last night.

Kevin   A shoelace?

Monica   It's a friendship bangle. (*Gets photos out.*) Look. That's them. The one on the left's Colin, the one on the right's Vince. We're going to have a reunion on Monday.

Kevin   They're a bit old for you, aren't they?

Monica   I think one of the most interesting things about foreign travel is you really let your barriers down.

Kevin   How old are they?

Monica   I don't know, but they've been together eighteen years. Eighteen years! I said, 'I've gotta hand it to you guys. You're setting a really good example to younger lesbians, gay men, transgendered and questioning people.'

Kevin   They look like the fucking Chuckle Brothers. (*Handing photo back.*) Are you still a dyke?

Monica   Yeah!

Kevin   But have you slept with a bird yet?

Monica   Do I have to pass a test or something? Being a lesbian's not like driving a car, you know.

Kevin   Well, you'd pass the written but I won't hold me breath for your practical.

Monica   And what if I slept with a woman in Mykonos?

Kevin   No you never! You never! I don't believe it!

Monica   Why is that so incomprehensible to you, Kev?

Kevin   Did she have a name? Or was it anonymous? In a lezzie back room.

Monica   Don't tar me with your brush, Kev.

Kevin   So where was it?

Monica   Look, I'm not saying I did, right?

Kevin   So you're still a lesbo virgin?

Monica   How's Tony? I've been so worried about him. I almost phoned him from Mykonos.

Kevin   He seems to be bearing up.

Monica   I was thinking about him non-bloody-stop. Poor Tonio. It's like his right arm's been wrenched off. The next few years are gonna be so tough for him. Facing the future. All alone. Every time I think about it I just crumble. I've gotta be strong. If only for him.

Kevin   He doesn't have to be alone. He's got us.

Monica   Yeah. Yeah. Oh, God, you can be really sweet when you want to. Yeah he's got us. And how's Mary?

Kevin   (*tuts*)   Don't ask.

Monica It can't be easy for her, Kevin.

Kevin It isn't easy for any of us.

Monica True, but there's different issues if it's your own kid. She carried him for nine months, don't forget. D'you know how many weeks that is? It's something like thirty-six. Maybe if you had a child you'd understand.

Kevin Oh yeah and that's really likely.

Monica I'm gay. Does that mean I can't have kids?

Kevin I'd be a crap dad.

Kevin *squints up at the sky and yawns.*

Monica Colin and Vince would love to father a child.

Kevin You didn't offer them your eggs!

Monica I'd love kids.

Kevin But you're on the Pill.

Monica I'm a lesbian, Kevin. It'd be pretty redundant.

Kevin You used to be on the Pill.

Monica God, I was having a really positive day 'til I came round here.

Kevin What you gonna be at this reunion? The main course?

Monica I wouldn't actually have to fuck them, you stupid idiot. I'd artificially inseminate myself with Colin's sperm.

Kevin Eugh! (*Looks her up and down.*) You'll need more than a fucking turkey baster. You'll need a good set o'bellows up you.

Monica D'you know one thing I realised in Mykonos?

Kevin You'll never be a size twelve?

Monica I hate sarcasm.

Kevin   You know where the door is.

Monica   It's a gate actually.

Kevin   You know where the gate is.

Monica   I'm waiting for Tony to get up. Now can I have your undivided attention please? Cos I've got something really major to tell you.

Kevin   Oh, *Mamma Mia* phoned while you were away. They want you to play the lead.

Monica *looks gobsmacked.*

Kevin   They didn't really.

Monica *gives him daggers.*

Kevin   Sorry. Was that really cruel?

Monica   Have a drink, Kevin. You're so much nicer when you're drunk.

Kevin   Why?

Monica   Sit down.

Kevin   You're a fucking control freak.

Monica *(dismissively)*   You sound like my therapist. Sit.

Kevin   I don't wanna sit.

Monica   OK, we'll stand.

Kevin   No. I wanna sit.

Kevin *sits.* **Monica** *shuts the French windows quietly.*

Monica   I met someone in Mykonos who really freaked me out.

Kevin   Who?

Monica   I didn't think it was him at first. I mean you don't expect to bump into someone from home in bloody Mykonos.

Kevin   Who?

Monica   Not that I really knew him as such. Depends on your definition of 'know', I guess.

Kevin   Oh, for God's sake, Mon, cut to the quick. Who?

Monica   Brett.

Kevin   Brett?

Pause.

Kevin   But you don't know Brett. None of us do.

Monica   I've seen photographs of him. When Frankie took him to Belgium he took a whole film. Thirty-six bloody pictures.

Kevin   Oh well. It's in the past, isn't it. He can't hurt no one now.

Monica   It just really freaked me out. Seeing him. You know.

Kevin   What did he look like?

Monica   Well . . .

Kevin   The way Frankie went on you'da thought he was shagging Michael Owen. Was he fit?

Monica   See for yourself.

She hands him a photo.

Kevin   Monica.

Monica   What?

Kevin   You've got your arm round him.

Monica   Yeah, my camera's got a self-timer.

Kevin   You mean you spoke to him?

Monica   Can I have that back please?

Kevin   I don't believe you.

Monica   Please.

Pause. **Kevin** *stares at the photo.*

D'you wanna hear some of my performance poetry?

Kevin   No.

Monica   I bought a biro from the beach taverna shop and wrote them on postcards. Tony!

Tony *comes out of the French windows, still in his dressing gown.* **Kevin** *puts the photo in his pocket.*

Tony   Hiya. Monica! You look gorgeous!

Monica   Oh, God I've really missed you, Antonio McBonio. Come here, you sexy beast.

Tony   God, you're looking great. Isn't she looking great, Kev?

Kevin (*Scottish*)   Aye, she looks fab.

Monica   Present! Open your present! It's not much. Mykonos really cleaned me out. It's a lot more expensive than it looks.

Kevin   How much was it? 50p?

Tony *too has unwrapped a mug.*

Tony   Oh, fab. Thanks a lot. I'll be able to . . . use it when I want a cup of tea. Or coffee. It's really versatile.

Monica   Look on the back. That's me. Little ole me. Well, less of the little. I was shovelling down moussaka like it was going out of fashion.

Kevin (*comparing mugs*)   Hang on a second. His says 'Friends For Ever', mine says 'Hi There!' D'you love him more than me or something? I feel like putting a fucking gun to me head!

Monica   Wanker!

She rubs **Tony**'s *arm and groans earnestly.*

How are you, Toe? You OK? You OK poppet?

Tony   I'm fine.

Monica   Ah! You're so brave. I'm so proud of you you know.

Tony   So come on. How was it? Tell all!

Monica   Yeah, it was a really cool headspace.

Tony   You didn't get bored?

Monica   I wrote poetry. My hotel had some really interesting shit in it.

Tony   Did you meet anyone nice?

Monica   Yeah, some really great guys from Stanmore. I've got to go there on Monday. We're having a reunion.

Kevin (*at the same time as she says reunion*)   Baby.

Monica *gives* **Kevin** *daggers*.

Monica   We're having a reunion.

Kevin (*at the same time again*)   Baby!

Monica   God, it's nothing definite, right? I don't know if I'm centred enough yet to bring some bloody kid into the world. I mean, I'm skint for starters. And my landlord's threatening to evict me.

Tony   Why?

Monica   Cos I didn't pay my rent when I was in Mykonos. Capitalist wankstain.

Tony   Are they photos?

Monica   Yeah. Did you know that Mykonos is Greek for windmill?

Tony   Let's see.

Monica   OK, but I've got to vet them.

Tony   Oh, Monica, we've all seen your tits before.

Kevin   The whole fucking country's seen your tits.

Monica   That documentary about breasts is up for a BAFTA.

Kevin   I've never seen so many saggy old mams in me life.

Monica   I don't show photographs to misogynists.

Tony   I'm not a misogynist, show me.

Monica   OK, but I have to vet them. I did some nude sunbathing and I've got some issues about who I expose my labia to. That's me with clothes on with Colin and Vince. Stanmore.

Tony   Talk me through this nasty blouse?

Monica   Oh, Colin and Vince bought it for me. I think they were having a bit of a giggle.

Tony   God, I can't abide T-shirts with slogans on.

Kevin   What does it say? Learner Lesbian?

Monica   Kev. You're starting to do my brain in!

Kevin   Let's see, what does it say?

Tony   'You can't keep a good woman down.'

Kevin   You can if you hold her head under the water long enough.

Monica   Give me that. Give it to me.

She snaps the photo out of **Tony**'s *hand. Grabs her bag.*

I'm outta here!

Kevin   You are the weakest link. Goodbye!

She takes a sip of her tea and then throws it over **Kevin**. *She exits via the back gate.*

Tony   Oh, I've only just mopped this!

Kevin   Stupid fucking bitch!

Tony *goes inside to get the mop.* **Monica** *comes back in.* **Kevin** *goes inside to wipe down.* **Tony** *comes out and mops up.*

Tony   Get out my way, I'll do that.

Monica   He gives gay men such a bad name you know. It's dangerous spouting bullshit like that. I know he only does it to wind me up, but it's no excuse. (*Shouts in the direction of the house.*) Wanker!

Tony   Keep your voice down. Jesus! I'm surrounded by bloody kids.

Tony *goes inside.* **Monica** *looks for the photo of her and Brett.* **Kevin** *comes out.*

Kevin (*Scottish*)   Tony says I've gottie apologise to yee.

Monica (*hushed*)   Where's my fucking photograph, you cunt?

Kevin (*hands it over*)   You wanna rip that up.

Monica   Oh, stop worrying. Tony doesn't know what he looks like. Tony doesn't even know he exists.

Tony *calls from inside.*

Tony   Who?!

Monica *and* **Kevin** *look back towards the house.* **Monica** *is shitting herself.*

Monica   What?

Tony   Who don't I know exists?

Monica   Oh, it's not important.

Tony *comes out.*

Kevin   Tell him.

Monica   Kevin!

Kevin Well, I will then. She's tryina set you up on a date, Tony. I told her it was too soon. He ain't gonna want another fella yet. You stupid fucking bitch!

She's a bit taken aback by his lie, and his attitude. She comes back at him.

Monica I know it's too soon, you vulgar cockney twat! (*To* **Tony**.) I just happened to mention someone gay in passing. And he's got them married off to you already! (*To* **Kevin**.) You twisted sick psychopath!

Kevin You were going on and on and on about how fantastic they were and how they really got off on the Scottish accent, you boring beached whale!!

Tony Who? Who are you talking about?

Kevin Yes, do remind me again Monica. I've already forgotten – it was so boring.

Monica Oh, just someone who comes in the caff.

Tony Does he have a name?

Kevin Yes, do tell, Monica. We're all ears.

Monica Of course he has a name. Randolf.

Kevin *laughs.*

Kevin Randolf?

Tony Well, thanks for the concern. But. Well, maybe I don't need to meet someone new.

Kevin That's exactly what I said. Frankie's only been dead six months! God, Mon, you're so insensitive!

Monica I just mentioned that he liked Scottish accents. That's all. I wouldn't set you up with anyone, Tony, I know it's wholly inappropriate.

Tony I mean, maybe I already have met someone.

Monica What?

Kevin   You're joking!

Monica   Really?

Tony   Why d'you think I went back to bed? I'm shagged.
Literally.

Monica   Right. Oh I see. You've had sex with someone.
God, is that all?

Kevin   You pulled down that vile pub?

Tony   Aha.

Kevin   You vile slut, Antony Graham. What are you like?!
Eugh, was he septic?

Tony   No, you cheeky bastard.

Kevin   When did he get off? I'll have to disinfect the
house.

Tony   About five minutes ago.

Kevin   It weren't Billy the barman, was it? He gave me
lice.

Tony   No.

Kevin   Well, who was it then?

Tony   No one you know.

Kevin   Good in the sack? Did he break your back?

Monica   Why does everything have to be measured by
sex, Kevin? You're such a stereotypical gay man, you do my
head in.

Tony   Well, aren't you happy for me?

Monica   Sure.

Kevin   If you're happy I'm happy.

Monica   Ditto.

Tony   Good.

Pause.

'Are you seeing him again Tony?' Yes, thanks for asking. We're gonna go clubbing tonight.

Kevin   Eugh, do you have to drone on about your vile trade. So you got a fuck last night. So what?

Tony   He wasn't vile.

Kevin   You don't hear me banging on about last night's meat, morning noon and night, do you?

Tony   No.

Kevin   No, cos I'm not boring.

Tony   No, cos you can't remember.

Monica   Er . . . guys? Can I ask something? Are you ready for this?

Tony   For what?

Monica   Another relationship?

Tony   Monica?

Monica   Toe?

Tony   Are you ready for a slap?

Kevin   Attaboy, Tony!

Monica   Tony!

Tony   Am I not allowed to meet anyone else? I thought yous two'd be really happy for me.

Monica   I am happy for you.

Kevin   I'm delirious.

Tony   I wish I could fucking believe you.

Kevin   What you worried about us for? It's your life.

Monica   Yeah. (*Directed at* **Kevin**.) I think it's really cool actually. Way to go, Toe!

Kevin   I haven't got a problem with it at all. I mean it's not like we're Mary, is it?

Monica   Oh, God! Don't tell her. I mean, it doesn't sound that serious.

Kevin   Monica! Are you encouraging Tony to lie?

Monica   Lies can be really positive, yeah? If you're . . . like . . . protecting someone.

Tony   And what if it is serious?

Monica   It's not.

Tony   Were you there?

Kevin   She was probably peering through the window, bringing herself off.

Monica   I think that's your department, Kev actually. Oh, come on, Tony. One night? Serious? Pur-lease!

Tony   Anyway, it's not like I tell Mary my deepest darkest thoughts.

Kevin   It's none of her business Tony. I wish she'd just give it a rest. Frankie wasn't even that close to her.

Tony   I know.

Mary *comes crashing in through the back gate. She is carrying a casserole dish in a plastic bag.*

Mary   Who, darling? I could hear your voices. Seemed silly to knock.

Monica   Mary! God, I've really missed you!

Mary   Who weren't our Frankie close to?

Kevin   Oh, you don't know her.

Mary   I know all Frankie's friends.

Tony   Oh, we're talking about someone else. Someone from down the pub.

Mary Who? Was she at the funeral?

Tony No.

Mary Oh well, some friend!

Monica I know. She's a fucking bitch guy!

Mary Oh, I hate that. Don't you hate that, Kevin?

Kevin I fucking loathe it, Mary, I'm so glad you asked me.

Mary You have a nice time on your travels, Monica? Oh, it's lovely to have you back. That path could do with a sweep. Don't do it now darling. Only popped round to bring you this. I can't stop. I made it for me lady with the leg but she turned her nose up at it. I thought, 'I bet Tony'll have that,' so I phoned you at Harvey Nicks.

Tony Oh, I didn't have to go in in the end. His shingles disappeared miraculously.

Mary I said, 'Is Tony in darling?' She goes 'Oh he ain't in today.' I goes, 'I'm glad. You're working him too hard as it is.' She just laughs. I thought, don't you fucking laugh at me. I said, 'How's that other lad's shingles then, darling?' She goes, 'Which other lad?' I said, 'Call yourself a manager!' and hung up.

She has produced a casserole dish.

Tony Mary, I'm not supposed to take personal calls at the shop.

Mary Well, I wanted to know where I could give you this. I thought, well, if you're up Knightsbridge all afternoon I could pop along. I've got me travelcard, seems a shame to waste it.

Kevin What is it? Eugh, it's got egg in it.

Tony (*has a look*) It's a Mary Special.

Mary   Frankie's favourite. Pasta, condensed tomato soup, tin o'tuna, tin o'peas, egg. I left the crisps out, darling cos I know you ain't enamoured. I'm not gonna eat it. You can have it with a little salad or a baked potato. Mind you, that might be a bit starchy. Where was it you went again, Monica? Greece, wannit?

Monica   Mykonos.

Kevin   It's Greek for windmill.

Mary   Bet it's nice to be home though. Always nice to get back to your own toilet.

Monica   You can't throw paper down Greek toilets.

Mary   Lovely. You taken your pills today, Tony?

Tony   No.

Mary (*slaps him*)   What've I told you?

Tony   Yes, I have taken my tablets, Mary. You've asked me three times already! What d'you want me to do? Overdose?

Mary   Well, pardon me for taking an interest! You were always moaning that Frankie never took an interest. I'm only trying to reshake the balance.

Monica   They have little bins and you stick it in there.

Kevin   Stick what?

Monica   The loo roll.

Mary   What?

Kevin   What are you on about, Monica?!

Monica   They don't let you throw toilet paper down the toilet.

Mary   Who don't?

Monica   The Greek authorities. You can get into real trouble for it.

Mary   What, they have someone standing over you while you're doing your dirties? That's fucking disgusting!

Monica   No. There's just like . . . a little bin there.

Mary   Oh, that's really hygienic. What if you've got company?

Monica   I've got you a present actually.

Mary   Here, she's bought you a bloody bin, Tony!

Monica   I was going to leave it here for you.

Mary   Me, darling?

Monica *hands her a gift-wrapped present.*

Mary   Oh.

She bursts out crying.

Oh, you didn't have to do that, darling. You shoulda saved your money.

Kevin   You ain't seen it yet. She give us cups.

Mary   Oh, it's too beautiful to open. Oh, you're all so good to me. I dunno why, I'm such a burden. Oh, you open it for me, Kevin. I ain't got me glasses on. Don't rip it darling, I'll use that paper at Christmas. Oh, you shoulda saved your money, Monica. Oh, she's a good girl. You're all good people. I dunno what I'd do without you.

Kevin *has unwrapped a sarong.*

Mary   Oh, isn't that stunning? That is stunning. Look at that. Oh, will you look at that, Tony? You can say what you like about their toilet facilities, but the Greeks do a lovely line in scarves.

Monica   It's a sarong.

Mary   No! Is it?

Kevin   Put it on.

Monica   Yeah.

Mary   What do I do with it?

Kevin   Come here.

Kevin *ties it on her.*

Mary   You cleaned your teeth yet, Kevin?

Kevin   Yeah.

Mary   You wanna suck on a Trebor. Oh, Monica, you've got an unusual eye, intya? Eh? Look at me like I'm on Camber Sands. Oh, this is very exotic. Oh, come here, you. (*Kisses* **Monica**.) I'm gonna keep this on I am.

Kevin   You look like David Beckham.

Mary   Well, he's a lovely dresser.

Monica   It's really versatile.

Mary   Isn't it? Isn't it? It'd make a lovely picnic rug. Or a baby's blanket. You seen Dodgy Rog, yet Kev?

Kevin   Give us a chance.

Mary   My arthritis, Monica. Fucking nightmare. So did you have a little holiday romance in Mykonos, babe? Meet a nice Greek man with a boat?

Kevin   Monica's a dyke.

Mary   Fucking load o'rubbish.

Monica   I am, Mary.

Mary   Yeah, well, I'm a lesbian an' all then.

Monica *shrugs as if to say it's cool.*

Mary   You'll have to get me down them lady bars. Find meself a nice lady in a bowler hat like in that film.

Kevin   Which film?

Mary   Beryl Reid and Susannah Whatsit.

Kevin   *The Killing of Sister George?*

Mary   Ooh, that's a sinister picture. Innit though, eh? Eh? Put the willies up me, that did. 'Ere, there was that movie set in Greece. She was in it. That actress. Shirley Valentine. Oh, I like that Shirley Valentine. She takes a good part.

Kevin   Pauline Collins?

Mary   That's it. That's a lovely picture. You seen *Pauline Collins* Mon? It's a lovely picture. You got that in your video shop, Kevin?

Monica   I went to the beach where they filmed that. That's where I met . . . people.

Mary   No! Was it lovely?

Monica   It's a bit touristy.

Mary   That's me that film.

Monica   Mykonos has all together become very touristy.

Mary   Like Soho, innit? What's the matter with you, Tony? Cat got your tongue?

Tony   No law against being quiet, is there?

Mary   You staying in tonight, Tony?

Tony   No, I'm going to Trade.

Mary   Lovely. I'm going up me club wi'Rose.

Monica   Which one's Rose again?

Mary   Used to be in the pub trade so she likes a bit o'that. (*Mimes drinking.*) Her fella went blind with his sugars. That's no way to lose your sight.

Tony   Is she the one who's the terrible gossip? Frankie said she was a scream.

Mary   Swears blind her fella's got a roving eye. But how can he? I'd get rid tomorrow, Tony, but she needs me see. Are they your holiday snaps, Monica?

Monica   Kind of.

Mary   Got any of that beach?

Monica   No.

Mary   Oh well, don't bother getting them out. Look at the fucking time! I'm nipping over St. Clements cos him upstairs got sectioned again. I only know cos his wife popped a note through. She's an angel, only she can't visit him today cos she's gone up Salisbury for a christening. I thought they only done them of a Sunday. Maybe they're Jewish, eh. You had any luck on the job front, Monica?

Monica   No.

Mary   Oh, that's a shame. You're Julie Andrews waiting to happen. See ya! Don't get up. Bye then.

She leaves.

Tony   I'm gonna get in the bath.

Tony *exits.*

Monica   God. So. What do you make of that, Kev?

Kevin   You're nothing like Julie Andrews.

Monica   About Tony's news!

Kevin   Well, good. I'm happy for him. It's his life.

Monica   Yeah, me too. It's great, isn't it? Yeah, really great.

He looks at her.

Blackout.

Scene Four

Sunday morning.

Kevin *is watching over the barbecue, which he has heated up. He puts some sausages and some bacon on it.* **Monica** *sits with two suitcases, an empty birdcage, a bin bag and a boogie box.* **Kevin** *is* *wearing sunglasses and a hat, which he takes off at some point in the scene, before* **Iggy**'s *arrival.*

Monica   Is Tony in bed?

Kevin   No, he ain't back from church yet.

Monica   Church?

Kevin   Trade. He's just phoned, he's on his way home. Told me to get some breakfast on. Said he's got company.

Monica   I'll pay you back for the cab as soon as I get paid. Are those Linda McCartney's?

Kevin   No, they're fresh.

Monica   You know. If this was America, right, I'd probably own a gun. They're like mobile phones over there. Everyone's got them. And I'd have pointed it straight between the eyes. And shot him. Dead.

Kevin   Who?

Monica   My landlord. Ex-landlord. Are these yours?

She helps herself to a cigarette from a packet on the table. She lights up. **Kevin** *rolls his eyes.*

Kevin   Help yourself.

Monica   Great. I haven't got a fucking girlfriend. I haven't got a fucking job. And now I haven't got a fucking home.

Kevin   Have they sacked you from the caff?

Monica   That's not a job. I'm a fucking actress!

Kevin   You can say that again. You're not thinking of stopping here, are you?

Monica   In your dreams, Kevin! No, Cora from the café, her flatmate Rafferty's gone trekking in Nepal. So she's going to put me up. Only she's doing her shift at the café 'til five so I can't go round 'til then. God, I had such a good chill in Mykonos and now this.

Kevin   Well, maybe you shoulda stayed put and paid your rent rather than splashing out on two weeks in Greece.

Monica   I've been depressed. I had to get away to find me again.

Kevin   Well, you didn't find you, did you? You found Brett.

Pause. **Kevin** *continues cooking.* **Monica** *sits.*

Kevin   What was he like?

Monica   I wasn't going to talk to him. When he walked into that bar. I couldn't take my eyes off him. I didn't fancy him.

Kevin   Well, obviously. You're a dyke.

Monica   I was thinking. Oh my God, it's him. And I just kept staring. Everyone else was staring at the sunset. The Kastro Bar, it's this bar where you go to watch the sunset. Huge great picture windows. The view's amazing. It's like this big round orange ball of flame and fire, just like . . . dropping into the horizonesque watery ocean. He ordered a strawberry daiquiri and then lit up a Camel Light. And he looked so vulnerable. And this classical music was playing. I felt like I was in a Caravaggio painting or something. Staring at this vision who looked like a rent boy. Then Colin and Vince started debating what music was playing and I said I thought it was the theme music from *The Mission*. And they said who was in that. And I said . . . Liam Neeson and Jeremy Irons.

Kevin   Oh get the fuck on with it.

Monica   And when I looked back . . . he'd gone. The waiter came with his Strawberry Daiquiri. *Malaka.* I said to the guys. 'That's what we should call our baby girl. *Malaka.*' Well, they just burst out laughing. Apparently it's Greek for wanker.

Kevin   But you spoke to him. You had your arms round him.

Monica   The next day I went to Super Paradise Beach. Yeah, me and seven million others. And who comes and lies on the lounger next to me?

Kevin   Fancy a spot in the shade did he?

Monica   It was like Frankie was sending me a sign or something. There must have been five hundred sun loungers on that beach, and he chose . . . Weird. So I spoke to him.

Kevin   Fuck me, that is weird.

Monica   He said he wasn't having that good a time in Mykonos. I said, 'Yeah, it's windy, isn't it?' and then he just came out with it. He and his boyfriend had always wanted to come. But his boyfriend had died. And so he was . . . doing it for him, so to speak.

Kevin (*incredulously*)   He called Frankie that? His boyfriend?!

Monica   Well, to Brett he was. OK to us he was Tony's. But to Brett. Brett was in love with Frankie. Frankie was living with someone else, but Brett was in a relationship with him all the same.

Kevin   Did you ever let on that you were a mate of Frankie's?

Monica   No. We were never bosom buddies. I only bumped into him about three times.

Kevin   So. He's going round thinking he was the love of Frankie's life? And what does he think Tony was? The bit on the side?

Monica   He loved Frankie.

Kevin   Shut up. He's just some little scally Manc you met on holiday who shagged our mate a few times.

Monica   Brett didn't even have a chance to say goodbye.

Kevin   Frankie got struck by lightning, Monica! None of us got a chance to say goodbye!

Monica   The first he heard that Frankie'd died was a message from Mary on his answerphone.

Kevin   Mary knew Brett?

Monica   Mary phoned everyone in Frankie's Filofax and let them know. Brett was in under 'Col the Carpenter'. Code name. Brett got in one night to a message on his answerphone saying Frankie McAdam wouldn't be needing any more carpentry. What an image. Yeah?

Kevin   You should write a poem about it.

Monica   I have. D'you wanna hear it?

Kevin   Life's too short.

Monica   Why do you always have to be so horrible to me, Kev?

Kevin   Force of habit.

Monica   You used to be really cool with me when we did the pub quizzes. You were always complimenting me on my knowledge of contemporary politics.

Kevin   You know your Bush from your Gores I'll give you that.

Monica   I remember the exact day you started being horrible to me.

Kevin   The minute we met?

Monica   That night at Marvellous. In the toilets. When I told you your feelings for Tony would never be reciprocated.

Pause.

Kevin   What feelings? What are you talking about?

Monica   Oh, face it, Kev, you've always carried a torch for Tony.

Kevin   Don't be daft! Frankie was my best mate!

Monica   You were always threatening to tell Tony about Frankie and Brett, and don't think I don't know why!

Kevin   Because I thought he had a right to know!

Monica   Because you thought they might split up and you'd get Tony to yourself.

Kevin   That's bollocks! So why didn't I tell him then?

Monica   Because you liked the idea of it. And were too scared of the reality.

Kevin   You're fucking mental, you are. I've been living with him for six months. Don't you think I woulda come on to him by now? If I was mad about him.

Monica   Haven't you?

Pause. **Monica** *laughs.*

Kevin   Of course I fucking haven't. Why? Has he said something?

Monica   You've always tried it on with Frankie's boyfriends, Kev. You try it on with everyone.

Kevin   I just get pissed, that's all. And when I get pissed I don't know what I'm doing. I ain't tried it on with Tony. He woulda said something. Has he said something, Monica?

Monica   No.

Kevin   I've gotta stop drinking. And I have. I didn't have a drink last night. I'm sick of finding meself in strange places at eight o'clock in the morning. Standing on the doorstep with me shoes on the wrong feet wondering how I got home. Losing me fucking bag. Losing me fucking memory. Getting flashbacks of people and lines of coke and rowing and . . . not knowing whether I've dreamt it or done it.

Meeting people in the clubs who reckon they've had a big
night out with you three weeks ago, and you don't know
them from Adam. Or fellas coming up saying 'You were
fucking rude to my boyfriend last week. He does not look
like Gary Glitter.' And you look at the boyfriend. And
they're right, he doesn't. Except for the fact he's got black
hair. And then you remember singing 'Leader of the Gang'
on a fucking table. And being vile. But convinced at the
time you were hilarious. And other people saying, 'Ah,
you're a lovely drunk.' When you know in your heart of
hearts what they mean is: You're so vile it's entertaining.

Monica   Is that why you stayed in last night?

Kevin   Kind of. And I didn't really want to meet Tony's
fella off me head.

Monica   It's weird, isn't it.

Kevin   I haven't laid a finger on Tony, Monica. If I had
I'd remember.

The back gate opens and **Tony** *comes in, off his tits.*

Tony   What's all this stuff? Is it more presents? Oh,
Monica, you didn't have to!

Tony *goes into the living room as she speaks and then reappears with
a picnic rug or blanket and goes about spreading it out on the decking.*

Monica   Oh it's just some of my stuff. I'm taking over
Rafferty's room at the commune.

Tony   Guess who was in the club. You'll never guess who
came to the club!

Kevin   Your new life partner? Well, where is he?

Tony   That bastard never turned up.

Off, we hear **Mary** *coming up the path.*

Mary   Where's he gone? (*Louder.*) Where've you gone?

Tony   We're out here!

Mary *comes through wearing her sarong.*

Kevin   I don't fucking believe it.

Mary   Put some sounds on, guy. Rose! Where's Rose?

Rose *comes in. She is tiny and splattered. She wears a summer dress with red wine down the front.* **Monica** *gets a CD out of her bag and puts it on her boogie box. It's Abba. She sits and sings along quietly to it, though with real feeling.*

Rose   I'm here.

Mary   Thought I'd lost you. Weren't that cab driver lovely?

Rose   Oh, he's a diamond. Oh yeah, d'you know who he puts me in mind of, Mare? Whatsisname. Used to be relief cellar man at the Elusive Camel. He had a terrible life. His Sharon was born with her pelvis back to front and no genitalia.

Mary   Get us a cup o'tea going. Me neck thinks me throat's been cut.

Rose   All her intestines was hanging out her stomach like a string bag. It's no life, is it?

Tony   Sod tea. Shall I raid the drinks cabinet?

Kevin   D'you want a bacon butty, girls?

Mary   Yeah, I've got the munchies.

Rose   I hope you're hygienic. All your meat's in the danger zone. I had to do a course when I ran the pub. Hygiene. We done lunches. Basic. Type o'thing Barbara Windsor does.

Tony *goes indoors.*

Mary   Someone roll a spliff.

Kevin   So you went to Trade, Mary?

Mary   Well, we was only round the corner. Down the Blind Beggar, as was. What's it called now, Rose?

Rose   I forget.

Mary   Anyway it was a bit of a late one there, so when they chucked out, she wanted another one, so I said, 'Why not try Trade?' I knew Tony was gonna be there. Nice, wannit, Rose?

Rose   Loud.

Kevin   Have you taken drugs, Mary? Popped a few pills?

Mary   Kevin! This is the one I told you about, Rose. Cheeky monkey, you are. Cheeky monkey!

Rose *starts tickling* **Kevin**.

Rose   Yeah, I thought it might be you. You've got a twinkle, int ya? What's going on behind them eyes you dirty bugger?! (*Giggles like a schoolgirl.*)

Mary   Ah, they all loved my baby there. Said he was a king among doormen.

Rose   Mare. I was out of order earlier. I know it. I'm sorry, everybody, if I offended but. You know. I don't want these fuckers chatting to me just cos I'm old. And that was the vibe I was getting.

Tony (*from inside*)   Rose knows loads o'famous people, don't you, Rose?

Mary   Well she used to run this pub near Victoria Bus Station so celebrities were always popping in en route to various destinations.

Kevin   Who's the most famous person you've ever met?

Rose   Salvador Dali.

Monica   Who?

Tony *comes out with a selection of drinks. He puts them down on the blanket. He has plastic beakers.*

Mary   I didn't like that fella you were speaking to by the toilets, Tony. He was all over you like a rash. I had a word. I said, 'Listen, love. He's grieving. Back off.' Well you are.

Tony   Brandy and coke?

Kevin   Please.

Rose (*to* **Kevin**)   You're making a right pig's ear o'that. Leave it to the professionals.

Kevin   No, you're all right, I'll do it.

Rose   Give it here! I've gotta do something or me hands'll seize up.

*She elbows **Kevin** out of the way and takes over the cooking.*

Mary   There was a lot of men in there tonight had their eye on you.

Kevin   So you were stood up, Toe?

Tony   Aye I was. I was supposed to meet him in there about midnight. He never showed. Searched high and low for him.

Mary   Who's this, darling?

Tony   Just a friend really.

Mary   Oh, it's good to have friends. You gotta be careful though. There's a lot of people out there who'll just want you for your money. Int that right, Ro?

Rose   'Ere, remember that Jap who was always sniffing around me?

Tony   Mary. It's obviously escaping your notice, but. I have no money.

Mary   You've got this lovely flat!

Rose   Made out he'd invented the wok, when they came all the rage in the eighties. Turned out he didn't have a pot to piss in.

Tony   Anyway it was only a friend, so there's nothing to worry about.

Mary   So why d'you search high and low for him?

Tony   Cos I wanted to see him.

Mary   Oh. That's nice. It's a great thing, friendship. It's great, isn't it, Monica?

Monica   Yeah it's the best.

Mary   Innit great, Kev?

Kevin   D'you know what it is, Mary? It's a tonic.

Mary   Ah! My Frankie had some lovely friends, didn't he, Rose?

Rose   Mmm, not half. Mind you they had nice friends.

Mary   Who?

Rose   This lot singing.

Monica   Abba?

Rose   When they come in the Elusive Camel, their mates were so respectful of me.

Monica   What did they drink?

Rose   Abba? Pernod and black.

Mary   Oh, shut up, Rose. It weren't the real Abba. It was that Abba tribute band. Yabba Dabba Doo. They doubled as the Flintstones.

Rose   They weren't, they were the real thing!

Mary   Oh, shut up. Were they Swedish?

Rose   No they were from Tunbridge Wells! I told you they were from Tunbridge Wells! I told that journalist!

Mary   Exactly! And what did he do? Laugh! (*About the joint.*) Fucking hell, that's strong.

Rose   Wash your mouth out. You're worse than Fern Britton. (*To the others.*) She's got a mouth on her. Cunt this, cunt that. I said to her, 'You don't speak like that on *Ready Steady Cook*! I think you should stick to halves!'

Mary   It wasn't Fern Britton! (*To the others.*) She's deluded.

Rose *leaves the confines of the barbecue with her sausage tongs and approaches* **Monica**.

Rose   What you staring at?

Monica   Me? Nothing.

Rose   I remember your mother. She threw a mean dart.

Monica   My mother doesn't play darts.

Rose   Oh, and why's that? Cos she broke her arm? And I suppose she told you she broke it falling on the ice? And I suppose you believed her. You silly whore.

Monica   Sorry?

Mary   Ro!

Rose   It was Big Alice Diamond what broke it cos she grassed up the Forty Thieves. Oh, the Old Bill said she was singing like they'd given her fucking canary seed once she got started. Dropped everyone right in it. Thanks a bunch!

Monica   My mother's called Phoebe.

Mary   D'you wanna have a dance, Tony?

Tony   No thanks, babe.

Kevin   Ah, it's a shame you got stood up, Tony. Are you gutted?

Mary   It was only a bloody little friend Kevin. Who gets upset over a fucking little friend? Eh? He lost his lover less than a year ago. What's missing one little inconsequential friend compared to that? He's got a garden full of friends here.

Rose   Well, I wouldn't call it a garden, all wood and concrete. When I was a girl you'd grow spuds in a plot like this. Is this streaky? I haven't got my specs on.

Kevin   I don't know why you don't just tell her.

Mary   Tell me what? What?!

Kevin   Well, maybe the fella he was going to meet was more than just a friend.

Mary   I don't understand what you're getting at, Kevin.

Tony   Kevin!

Kevin   Maybe Tony actually quite likes him.

Mary   Frankie's only been gone six months. He ain't even cold, darling. Tony ain't ready yet, darling. Are you, darling?

Tony   No, darling.

Mary   See?

Tony   Kevin gets his wires crossed sometimes.

Mary   Our Frankie used to say that. He'd say 'Mummy. Kev don't half get his wires crossed sometimes.' D'you remember, Ro?

Rose   No.

Kevin   I don't believe for one minute that Frankie ever called you Mummy, Mary.

Mary   Was you there?

Kevin   I was round your flat often enough when I was growing up. The nicest thing I heard him call you was 'Bitch'.

Pause. This throws everyone. **Kevin** *laughs to make light of it.* **Mary** *giggles, embarrassed.*

Mary   You cheeky monkey. Eh? You cheeky monkey.

Rose Cheeky monkey!

Monica Kev, that's bang out of order. Just because your relationship with your mum was dysfunctional.

Kevin Dysfunctional?

Monica It doesn't follow that everyone's relationships are fucked up.

Kevin What d'you mean, dysfunctional?

Monica Well, your mum was a smackhead, wasn't she? I'd have thought that would make for a pretty dysfunctional relationship. I could be wrong.

Kevin Who told you that? She's weren't a smackhead. She weren't!

Mary Weren't she darling? You hundred per cent sure about that? You can tell me. I'm pretend family, darling.

Kevin No. (*To* **Monica**.) Fucking hell, you wanna reassess your attitude.

Mary That's why you lived with your old nan.

Kevin No.

Monica Well, sorry, right, but Frankie told me otherwise. He was obviously lying. Maybe she had a toke on a joint once. And by a process of Chinese whispers that turns into 'Oh God, did you know that Kevin's mum's on drugs?' Don't blame me, blame the gay community. Gossipy or what?

Tony Can we have something else on?

Rose You got any Badly Drawn Boy?

Mary What did you say, Monica?

Rose I knitted him that hat.

Monica Sorry?

Mary Did you call Frankie a liar?

Monica   Well . . .

Mary   A liar and a gossip?

Rose   That's her family all over. Stirrers.

Mary   When he ain't even here to defend hisself?

Rose   Don't tell her nothing!

Mary   Oh, that's really nice, that is, Monica. Tell me, Tony. Were you aware that my dead son was a liar and a gossip? Only Monica here reckons he was.

Tony   None of us are perfect, Mary.

Mary   Oh! So you'd agree? Anything else we wanna slag him off for while I'm here? Jesus, you won't even wait 'til me back's turned.

Kevin   He was a liar. About some things. We all lie.

Mary   That's a terrible accusation.

Kevin   No it's not.

Monica   Well, *somebody* told me your mum was a smackhead.

Mary   Oh, great, so pick on the person who ain't here to defend hisself to get the blame! Of course it's true. What else would explain your rottenness? Don't get me wrong, darling, I love you, you know I love you. But you are rotten at times, rotten.

Kevin   I don't believe this!

Tony   Can't we talk about something nice?

Kevin   My mum is nice! You're so full of shit, Monica!

Monica   I must have made a mistake. Sorry.

Mary   I hope so, darling. It ain't nice to hear about your dead son's negative aspects.

Monica   Look, Mary, I didn't mean to . . .

Mary   Mean to what, darling? Fuck me off? Well, you have.

Rose   D'you know who's lovely? Gargy Patel.

Monica   All I meant was . . .

Mary   D'you think it doesn't hurt? When I see horrible things written about queers in the papers? D'you not think every time I see an MP on the news spouting bollocks it don't cut through me like glass? 'My Frankie weren't like that,' I wanna scream. 'Come and meet my Frankie. He'll change your mind.' Only he can't now cos he ain't here. And every time someone's rude about gay lads on the box I take it personal. They're slagging off my son. And they didn't even know him. And you did. And yet you're more than ready to coat him.

Monica   All I said . . .

Mary   I heard what you said. Oh, Monica. Don't break my heart.

She falls into **Monica***'s arms and sobs her heart out.*

Rose   I love a nice Asian.

Mary   When you've got kids you'll understand.

Kevin   Funny you should say that.

Monica   Drop it, guy!

Kevin   Oh, am I not supposed to tell anyone?

Mary   Eh?

Kevin   Sorry.

Mary   You're not pregnant, are you?

Rose   I knew it. I thought she was pregnant, only I didn't like to say in case she was just . . .

Monica   I'm not pregnant.

Kevin   Yet.

Monica   Drop it, Kev!

Rose   Now I ain't saying she's fat. Cos she ain't. She's glowing. And a lot of people glow when they're pregnant.

Mary   I was like a fucking Belisha beacon, Monica. Do you want little babies, Monica? Did you hear that, Rose? I'm gonna be a grandma!

She starts to cry again.

Monica   Look, you know. My mind isn't made up or anything. I mean, it's a big step. I don't know if I'm up to it.

Mary   Oh, it's easy, Monica. It's easy. It's like riding a bike. Can you ride a bike? (**Monica** *nods*.) Have a baby, Monica. You'd make a lovely mum, you would. Wouldn't she make a lovely mum, Rose?

Rose   Dunno.

Monica   But it's really painful.

Mary   When they hurt you? I know, darling. But the pros outweigh the cons. Believe me, babe.

Monica   No, I mean, like . . . giving birth.

Kevin   Can you still die in childbirth?

Monica   I don't know. Shit, can you?

Kevin   Fingers crossed!

Rose   I like him.

Monica   I'm going to the toilet.

Kevin *is pissing himself.* **Monica** *runs inside.*

Mary   Who's she having a baby by, Kevin?

Kevin   A couple o'saddos she met on holiday.

Rose   Trollop. And her the size of a house.

Mary   That's my baby girl you're talking about.

Rose   Oh, listen to you. 'She's one of my kids!' Another one you've adopted to make you feel better about Frankie.

Mary   Nothing's gonna bring him back, Rose.

Rose   Good. Cos all he did was cause you heartache.

Mary   Is somebody rolling a spliff or not? Where's your dope box, Tony?

Tony   In the living room.

Mary *goes indoors.*

Rose   It's true. But she don't like the truth. Never did. Her and Rula Lenska.

Monica *comes out and heads for the back gate.*

Tony   Where are you going?

Monica   Out. I can't bear the smell of all this burning flesh.

Kevin   See you, lesbo!

Monica   Fuck off poufter.

Rose   Tell your mother she wants to learn to button her lip!

Monica *exits.*

Rose   Is she lesbian?

Kevin   She'd like to think she is.

Rose   Does her mum know? She'll go fucking spare.

Mary *comes to the French windows.*

Mary   Where's this bloody tin?

Tony (*to* **Kevin**)   Go and show her.

Mary (*to Rose*)   I'm not speaking to you.

Rose   No? Oh, that's a shame.

Kevin *goes inside with* **Mary**.

Rose   He was always breaking her heart, silly cow.

Tony   I know he was hardly an angel.

Rose   All she ever did when he was alive was moan about him.

Tony   Oh well. We all do things we regret in retrospect.

Rose   Dunno why you're defending her. She never had a good word to say about you. I had you down as a right monster.

Tony   What? What did she say?

Rose   How you was eating away at his money.

Tony   Me? Frankie was a fucking bouncer. I'm management material!

Rose   We all know he done funny things on the side. Bouncing never paid for this flat.

Tony   No, I did! We put it in Frankie's name cos I'm HIV. I'd never have got a mortgage.

Rose   She never liked that neither. Case you gave it to him. At first she thought you was making it up, to snare Frankie.

Tony   To snare him?

Rose   'Oh, he's always been a soft touch, my Frankie. Always been a glutton for a sob story. That boy's got him just where he wants him.'

Tony   Why on earth would me being HIV snare him? It'd put most people off.

Rose   Oh am I being out of order? You can tell me. I can take it.

Tony   No. No, you're not. You're telling the truth. If I'm to be honest I . . . My head's pretty screwed up right now. I'm such a coward.

Rose   What you scared of?

Tony   People not understanding me.

Rose   Oh, who gives a toss what other people think?

Tony   I don't understand me.

Rose   If I'da spent me life worrying what every fucker thought about me, I wouldn't have had half the fun I've had.

Tony   Why does she have this hold over me?

Rose   She makes people listen to her. And they do. Even if she is speaking crap. She used to tell people I was an alcoholic. It got back to me. I spread it round she had a false leg. Well it was when she was always wearing them suede ski-pants.

Tony   Did she say any of that stuff to Frankie? About me. Not trusting me.

Rose   That was all they used to row about. He came down the pub and had it out with her. 'Stop coating my Tony you interfering bitch! You ain't welcome round my house!' Looked like he was going to punch her. She was hiding behind me Golden Wonder.

Tony   He said she refused to come cos his dad wouldn't let her. She only started coming after he left her.

Rose   Siddie never stopped her going nowhere!

Tony   I wonder why he didn't just tell me.

Rose   Oh, he was probably trying to protect you. You know her problem? She didn't bond with him when he was a baby. Weren't her fault, the . . . (*Clicks fingers.*) didn't click. That's sad when that happens. There's someone coming up your back passage. (*Calls.*) Who is it?

Off, we hear **Iggy** *calling.*

Iggy   It's Iggy!

Rose   Iggy?

Tony   Oh fuck, is it?

Rose   Iggy? What sort of a name's that?

Iggy *comes in through the back gate.*

Iggy   All right, Tony?

Tony   What time d'you call this? I thought we were supposed to be meeting in the club?

Iggy   Better late than never.

Tony   This is Rose. This is Iggy.

Rose   Oh, it's you.

Iggy   Sorry?

Rose   Ever been down the Elusive Camel?

Iggy   Er, no.

Rose   Oh, well it ain't you then. What are you talking about? Keep an eye on breakfast. I'm gonna have a kip.

Rose *lies down on the sun lounger.* **Tony** *keeps an eye on the barbecue.*

Iggy   Are you trashed?

Tony   I looked all over for you.

Iggy   I'm a wanker. What more can I say? Did you cop for any one last night?

Tony   No. You weren't there.

Iggy   What's it got to do with me?

Tony   Woulda been a bit embarrassing now.

Iggy   I'd sit out here 'til he went away.

Tony   D'you want a drink?

Iggy   I'll have this. (*Takes drink off table.*)

Tony   It's not yours.

Iggy   Is now.

Tony   I should be really angry with you.

Iggy   What you gonna do? Hit me?

Tony   But I'm not. I'm too angry with someone in there.

Iggy   I don't mind if you're angry. I'd be angry. I'd hit you.

Tony   You? You're a scrawny little fucker.

Iggy   Is this yours? (*Puts **Kevin**'s hat on.*)

Tony   No. It's Kevin's.

Iggy   Chuck us them shades.

Tony   They're not yours either.

Iggy   I'm in disguise.

*He sits there in the hat and sunglasses that **Kevin** was wearing earlier. He sits there, facing the sun.*

I was gonna come down. But I went for a walk instead. Walked all over. Walked across that Tower Bridge. Felt like jumping off. Having a midnight dip.

Tony   Why?

Iggy   Don't you ever feel like doing mad things?

Tony   I once wrote to *Jim'll Fix It* asking to be the fifth member of Brotherhood of Man, but it's hardly staring madness in the face is it?

Rose *pipes up, still with her eyes shut.*

Rose   Isn't it?

Mary and Kevin appear at the French windows. Mary is proudly holding up a massive joint.

Mary   Look at the size o'that! Oh. Who's this then? We've got a visitor, Kevin.

Tony   This is Iggy. My new little friend.

Kevin   All right?

Mary   Iggy? Oh, that's unusual, innit?

Tony   The boy who stood me up.

Kevin   You're wearing my hat and glasses, mate.

Iggy   Sorry.

Kevin   Nah, keep them. For now.

Tony   Kevin, this is the beautiful Iggy.

Iggy   Oright, mate?

Tony   And Mary.

Iggy   Hi, Mary.

Mary   So you didn't come to the club last night.

Iggy   No.

Mary   It was fucking wicked. We was largin' it, wasn't we Ro? Rose, eh?

Iggy   You went to Trade?

Mary   I'm never out of that place. You're probably wondering who I am.

Tony   You're Mary. He's not deaf.

Mary   I'm Tony's mother-in-law.

Tony   As was.

Mary   You look tired, Tony. You should have a lie-down. He should have a lie-down. Tell him, Kevin.

Tony I'm fine, Mary. The elephant tranquillisers I took at three of the o'clock this morning appear to be kicking in.

Mary *looks very sad. She sits on the step up to the decking and rests her head on her hand, staring contemplatively at the ground.* **Tony** *rolls his eyes.*

Iggy You OK, Mary?

Mary I'll be all right in a minute.

Kevin What's the matter with you, Mary?

Tony As if we didn't know.

Mary Oh, I was just thinking. It's nothing. You all ignore me. I'll be fine. Eventually.

Iggy You look dead sad.

Mary I've lost me son.

Kevin She's so careless.

Tony *giggles.* **Mary** *gives* **Kevin** *daggers then looks back to* **Iggy**.

Mary I expect Tony's told you.

She reaches out and holds **Tony**'s *hand, not looking at him.*

Iggy Yeah he did.

Mary You'da liked him, darling. He was one of the best.

Iggy I'm sure. I'm sorry Mary.

Mary It was only six months ago. He ain't even warm.

Tony Cold!

Mary Cold. It's nice that Tony's got good friends. His heart's breaking every second of the day. Ain't that right, Tony? Takes a long time to get over someone like my Frankie, ain't that right, baby boy?

Tony (*sarcastically*) Years.

Mary *nods her head, sagely.*

Tony   May I have my hand back?

Tony *removes his hand from* **Mary**'s *grasp.*

Mary   You ever had a mum, Iggy?

Iggy   Yeah.

Mary   You treat her good, yeah?

Iggy   Yeah. I think so.

Mary   That's beautiful.

Tony   Actually, I think I will go to bed. Iggy?

Mary   Oh, I was just beginning to enjoy meself then.

Tony   Care to join me?

Mary   Don't go to bed, darling. We can all sit up and have a singsong. Does anyone know 'Edelweiss'?

Tony   We've been up all night. You're no spring chicken any more.

Mary *starts to sing 'Edelweiss'.*

Rose *sits up and joins in.*

Mary *gives* **Rose** *daggers.*

Mary   Did I ask you to join in?

Rose   I know her.

Mary   I've got a lovely voice. Coulda been professional. A gypsy once crossed my path with silver and said she seen big things for me in the opera.

Rose   Bollocks!

Rose *lies back down again.*

Tony   Maybe we should all call it a day.

Mary   Oh, Tony! I'm having too nice a time to go home.

Iggy   D'you live near?

Mary   No. I'd need to get the bus. What bout you?

Iggy   I'll walk you to the stop. I'm only round the corner.

Mary   Oh. So you ain't stopping neither?

Iggy   No.

Mary   Oh. Rose. Rose!

Rose *sits up again.*

Rose   She's another one with a mouth on her.

Mary   Rose, we're going.

Rose   I said, 'Bit of a comedown from jigging round that nunnery, you dirty strumpet.'

Mary   Rose, Tony wants his bed, darling, and Iggy's gonna walk us to the bus stop.

Rose   What about my breakfast?

Mary   Give us a kiss and tell me you love me, Tony. See you, Kev. Tell Monica bye, yeah?

Tony   See you. See you, Iggy.

Kevin   Bye then.

Iggy   I suppose you'll be wanting these.

He takes off the shades and hat.

Nice meeting you.

Kevin *gets the fright of his life when he sees* **Iggy**'s *face for the first time.*

Mary   Say goodbye, Kevin. Bloody hell, you're so rude.

She links **Iggy**'s *arm.*

What's your mum's name, darling?

Iggy   Denise.

Mary   Oh, that's a pretty name. She a bit on the young side?

Iggy *leaves with* **Mary** *and* **Rose**. *We hear them talking as they walk up the path.*

Iggy   Forty-three.

Mary   Oh, she's a baby. D'you hear that, Rose?

Rose   What?

Mary   Forty-three.

Rose   Who?

Mary   His mum. Denise.

Rose   Well, if she's anything like Denise Nolan she'll be lovely.

Mary   She's just a baby. And how old's your nan?

Rose   There's a bus. Leg it!

We hear them run off down the path. **Kevin** *and* **Tony** *sit there a while.*

Kevin   Where did you meet him?

Tony   The pub. Do I look disgusting or something?

Kevin   Where does he live?

Tony   Manchester. He's staying at a B&B round the corner. He couldn't bear to look at me for more than five minutes.

Kevin   What did he say his name was?

Tony   Why?

Kevin   He just . . . reminds me of someone.

Tony   Who?

Kevin   I dunno.

Tony   Don't you think he's cute?

Kevin   He's all right, yeah.

Tony   Please don't do a Mary on me.

Kevin   It's difficult, you know.

Tony   Why is it difficult?

Kevin   I dunno. It just is.

Tony   Come here.

He hugs **Kevin** *to him.*

Kevin   You'll maybe never see him again, eh.

Tony   Don't sound so fucking pleased.

Kevin   Stop touching me.

Tony   Why?

Kevin   Cos I can't fucking bear it!

Tony *lets* **Kevin** *go.*

Kevin   No. Don't stop.

Tony *hugs him again.* **Kevin** *closes his eyes and savours it.* **Iggy** *comes back in.*

Iggy   Am I interrupting something?

Tony   Darling!

Iggy   Well, that was easy. Bus was already there. She weren't happy, was she? I kind o'got the impression that she didn't want me knocking about with you. It was only a little white lie. Don't mind that, do you?

Tony   No. You played that really well didn't you? Who's a clever boy?

Iggy   Are you ready for bed yet?

Tony   Listen sweetheart, if I were gonna do anything, I need a shower. I've been dancing all night – certain parts of me are not smelling like roses. I won't be long. You keep an eye on my Iggy, Kev? And keep your mucky paws off. I'll be two ticks. (*To* **Iggy**.) He goes anywhere near you? Scream!

Tony *goes in.* **Kevin** *watches* **Iggy**. *He sits down and knocks back his drink.* **Kevin** *is staring at him. He shuts the French windows.*

Iggy   Have I got a welly on me head?

Kevin   What did you say your name was again?

Iggy   Iggy.

Kevin   Does anyone ever call you anything else?

Iggy   Like what?

Kevin   Like your real name?

Iggy   Ignatius?

Kevin   No. (*Beat.*) Brett.

Iggy *looks at* **Kevin**.

Blackout.

Act Two

Scene One

Sunday morning.

Kevin *and* **Iggy** *sitting there.* **Kevin** *is knocking back a drink. He's quite pissed now.*

Kevin   I've seen a photograph.

Iggy   People look alike. (*Takes a swig of drink.*)

Kevin   Don't you fucking drink that! What game are you playing?

Iggy   I'm not playing any . . . ! Who's this Brett fella?

Kevin   You can't pull the wool over my eyes!

Iggy   Was Frankie having an affair then?

Kevin   Hah! Did I say that?

Iggy   Does Tony know?

Kevin   No. Keep your fucking voice down!

Iggy   But you do. And you never told him. What sort of a friend are you?

Kevin   Not half as fucked up as you are. Shag the dead one, get the live one. You sick or something?

Iggy   I'm Ignatius. You're mistaken.

Iggy *makes to go in.* **Kevin** *bars his way.*

Kevin   Leave Tony alone.

Iggy   Why should I? What right have you got to tell me what to do?

Kevin   Because I'm a grown-up, you're a kid, and he's my mate.

Iggy   I dunno what the fuck you're talking about, mate. Now can I go in, or do I have to hit you?

Kevin   What d'you want? Money? I'll give you money. (*Goes in pockets.*) How much d'you want?

Iggy   What d'you think you are? The Mafia?

Iggy *tries to push past* **Kevin**.

Kevin   Leave him alone!

Kevin *wrestles him away from the door and on to the decking.* **Iggy** *easily brushes him off, as he is so pissed.* **Kevin** *sits on the decking and starts to cry. He gets up, sits at the table, trying to hide it.* **Iggy** *watches this.*

Iggy   You know, Tony was right about you. You're fucking barmy, mate. Listen. Let's not say owt about this to Tony. If Frankie was having an affair. He doesn't need to know, does he? And as I'm not this . . . Brett character. I'm gonna go in, and forget this conversation ever happened. You're drunk, Kevin.

Kevin   Drinking doesn't make me stupid, you prat!

Iggy   Well, it makes you fucking paranoid! What's the difference?

Kevin   Musta been strange. Meeting Mary. The woman who gave your lover life.

Iggy   Are you on tablets? I think you should take some.

Kevin   No I'm not on fucking tablets! For Christ's sake, where do you get off?

Iggy   Look, I don't want a slanging match. I just wanna be with Tony, yeah? I certainly don't wanna fall out with his mates.

Kevin   Why? Why are you doing this?

Iggy   I'm down for a couple o'days. I meet a guy in a bar. We have a bit of fun. I go home. There is no 'why' about it.

Kevin   Nobody stays in Dalston.

Iggy   It's cheap.

Kevin   Unlike you, you're free.

Iggy   Jealous?

Kevin   Of what?

Iggy   That I've got Tony?

Kevin   Why would I be jealous?

Iggy   You're just making up stories to try and get rid of me. Cos you want him for yourself.

Kevin   Why does everyone think I've got a thing for Tony?

Iggy   Well, you seem a bit obsessed with him.

Kevin   He's my friend.

Iggy   If you want. (*Makes to go in.*)

Kevin   Oi! I'm not some sad alcoholic because I'm in love with Tony! I'm a sad alcoholic cos I'm not in love with anybody. And what you're doing is fucked up!

Iggy   You're so wrong. About me.

Kevin   Brett was from Manchester.

Iggy   A lot of people are.

Kevin   You're the fucking image of him. You're his doppelgänger!

Iggy   Look. I'm sorry, but I'm not him.

Kevin   I hate all this.

Iggy   What?

Kevin   Lying. It's not right.

Iggy   So Frankie was seeing someone else?

Pause. **Kevin** *stares at* **Iggy**.

I won't tell Tony, if that's what you want.

Kevin   Yes.

Iggy   How long for?

Kevin   It doesn't matter.

Iggy   What a bastard.

Kevin   Sometimes I read things into things that aren't there. Stupid things. D'you know what I mean? And it all seems so real to me. I'm sat here and I'm convinced that you are this Brett geezer. Panicking about how I break it to Tony. I hate secrets. Listen to me. I get carried away sometimes. Great. I've told you something I should never have breathed to a soul. I can't tell Tony, but I can tell a complete stranger. I know you hardly know him and that. But you can see he's dead sound. You're not gonna tell him, are you? I think it's my guilty conscience.

Iggy   No, mate. I won't be telling him owt.

Kevin   Frankie treated him like shit, you know. And he just took it. Monica thought he was a fool. I thought he had dignity. I've never had a relationship. Not proper. I dunno what I feel any more. But I know this much. I ain't waiting for the grieving widow to turn round and tip me the wink. I just get confused cos I'm lonely. D'you ever get lonely?

Iggy   Come on, mate. Calm down.

Kevin   Do you?

Iggy   Yes.

Kevin   You're called Iggy, aren't you?

Iggy   Yes.

Kevin   You're not Brett, are you?

Iggy *shakes his head.* **Kevin** *sits there, crying.* **Iggy** *goes to get* **Kevin**'s *drink and hand it to him. As he does,* **Monica** *returns,* *carrying a large bag and putting her mobile phone away.* **Iggy** *has his back to* **Monica** *at first.*

Monica Hi, Kev! Look, I'm so sorry about earlier. Guess what? My really great friend Candice has just rung and there's this new musical and they're looking for really great black actresses who can . . .

Iggy *turns round to see who it is.* **Monica** *stands staring at* **Iggy**. *They stay staring at each other.*

Kevin Oh, this is Iggy. Tony's new . . . friend.

Pause.

Kevin The bloke Tony was going on about. Iggy. Stood him up last night. This is him. He's sound as a pound.

Monica What are you doing here, Brett?!

Pause.

Kevin What?

Iggy You two know each . . . ?

Kevin This is Iggy. It is, it's Iggy.

Iggy You're that bird from Mykonos.

Kevin You said. You fucking bastard!

He lunges at **Iggy**. *He gets* **Iggy** *in the eye.*

Monica Get off him! Kev, get off him! Oh God, he's really drunk.

Kevin It's him. The twat that Tony's been seeing.

Iggy (*to* **Monica**) Why didn't you tell me? I poured me heart out to you! (*Winces.*) Me fucking eye!

Monica Look. I never lied to you, Brett. I just . . . didn't tell you the truth.

Kevin I was right. I was fucking right. And you made me think . . . !

Monica   Oh, shut up, Kev, you're pissed.

Kevin   But . . .

Monica   Drop it, Kev!

Pause.

Iggy   Don't look at me like I'm a piece of shit. I don't have to explain myself to you.

Monica   Fine. So I take it Tony knows who you are?

Pause.

Iggy   You're just as much a liar as I am.

Monica   I didn't follow you to Mykonos!

Iggy   You should have told me.

Monica   Well, that's the pot calling the kettle black.

Iggy   I didn't plan this.

Kevin   What did you plan? Come and stay in Dalston just to visit his grave?

Iggy   And what's so barmy about that?

Monica   What's barmy is you're shagging his boyfriend.

Kevin   You can't tell him now. You've got to tell him but you can't tell him now. He's off his nut. It's not safe. You'll freak him out.

Monica   I don't quite believe this is happening. As if my life couldn't get any worse. You wouldn't believe the day I've had.

Iggy   I thought you were all right.

Monica   I am.

Kevin   She's one of the nicest people she knows.

Monica   How did you think you'd get away with it?

Iggy   Frankie said no one knew.

Monica Oh, he couldn't shut up about you. Not in front of Tony. Just.

Iggy I told you loads.

Monica I'm a good listener.

Iggy You don't give a shit about Tony. Neither of you do.

Monica I love Tony. Tony's, like, one of my closest pals.

Iggy So why didn't you tell him?

Monica I thought he'd never find out. What you don't know doesn't hurt you.

Iggy Well, he wouldn't, if you didn't tell him.

Monica Why, Brett?

Iggy All I wanted was to put flowers on Frankie's grave. Look at the flat he lived in from the outside. Go to the pubs he drank in. Look at it from my point of view. I loved him. And I didn't even know when his funeral was. All I get's a message on me machine saying. And Frankie didn't know any of my mates. So it's not like I can gab to them about him. I didn't know any of his. I just wanted to feel close to him. Then I meets a bloke in a pub and he chats me up. And he tells me his name, and I think . . . nah, can't be. Can't be. So I asks him what street he lives in. And I know. And he invites me back. For a coffee. But I know he wants to fuck me. Everyone wants to fuck me.

Kevin Bit full of yourself, aren't you?

Iggy Frankie never. He liked me for me. I'm not a cunt, Monica. You know that. So I thinks, will I? Won't I? Shall I go back? What do I do? So I says to Tony I need a crap. So I goes to the bog in the pub and I think, if I stay here. If I just stay here for half an hour, he'll fuck off. He'll think I've got off. So I sit there, on the bog. And I smoke a fag. I hears his voice. Asking me if I'm all right. I said, 'I've got the squits.' I'm thinking, if he thinks I've got a shitty arse he

won't want me to go back with him. He goes, 'I've got
Dioralyte back at my place.' This bloke ain't giving up.

Monica   You should have gone home.

Iggy   I wanted to see what Frankie's flat was like. I reckon
I can come back, have a drink, and get off. Have a quick
butcher's. So I've got a picture in me head. Then scarper.
Nobody's hurt nobody. And we come back. And he makes
me a Dioralyte. To stop me crapping. Only I'm not really
crapping, but I drink it anyway . . . and that makes me feel
ill. Well, he's not letting me go home now. He's gonna take
care of me. Next thing I know this guy's telling me about his
dead boyfriend. And he's my dead boyfriend. And I can't
tell him. I want to. I want to grab hold of him and say I
know exactly how you feel. I feel so close. Then I'm lying in
Frankie's bed and Frankie's boyfriend is making sure I'm
OK. And I think fuck it. Why shouldn't I stay? He'll never
know. I didn't set out to hurt Tony. Tony's all right. I can
see why Frankie was with him. And I hate meself that I
mighta come between Frankie and him.

Monica   If you didn't set out to hurt him, you'll just go
now.

Iggy   And what excuse would I give? I can't.

Kevin   Easy. Say the usual crap blokes say. You're not
ready for this. Christ, he can't be ready for this, won't be
like you're speaking a foreign language.

Monica   I knew something like this was going to happen.
I'm quite psychic. No, really. The way I kept bumping into
you in bloody Mykonos. I saw you at the Kastro Bar. You
ordered a drink and then left.

Iggy   How did you know?

Monica   I saw a photo of you. When you went to
Belgium. All those photos he took.

Iggy   Have you still got them?

Monica   He put everything with you on it. Photos.
Address books. Keepsakes. Letters.

Iggy   I never sent him letters. I sent him emails.

Kevin   He used to print them out and keep them.

Iggy   Did he?

Monica   If I could just finish! He put them all in left-
luggage at Paddington.

Iggy   Where are they now?

Monica   We don't know. .

Iggy   But there'd be a receipt? The ticket for the left
luggage. He'd have a ticket for that, wouldn't he?

Monica   He kept it in his wallet.

Iggy   And where's that? What if Tony found it?

Kevin   When Frankie died. The guy who. The guy who
stayed with him 'til the ambulance came. We don't know
who this guy was. And. The police seem to think he. Well,
they know. He went through Frankie's pockets. His wallet
was missing. And his house keys. Tony had to get the locks
changed.

Iggy   That's fucking sick. Robbing from a dead man? I
wish you'd told me you knew him. What were you thinking?

Tony *opens the French windows, dressed in a towel, fresh from the
shower.* **Iggy** *and* **Monica** *look round.*

Tony   Ah! My three pals bonding! This is what I like to
see. Isn't he gorgeous?

Monica   Yes but what a shame he's got to get off so
quickly. Oh shit. Sorry. You haven't told him, have you? I
put my size sevens in it again!

Tony   What?

Iggy   Tony. There's something I've gotta tell you. I've. I've gotta go back to Manchester tomorrow.

Tony   I thought you were going back on Tuesday?

Iggy   I know but. I found out today I've got a job interview Tuesday. So I need to get back up tomorrow. It's a pisser, innit?

Tony   Better make the most of you while I've got you then. Come on.

Tony *makes to head back in.* **Kevin** *and* **Monica** *are looking at* **Iggy**, *wondering what he is going to do.* **Tony** *looks back, wondering why he is not following.*

Iggy   That's the other thing. I've gotta phone the bloke about the job tonight. Well, he's phoning me at the B&B, so I've gotta get off.

Monica   I'm going to get a drink.

Kevin *shakes his head.* **Monica** *goes inside.*

Tony   What's the job?

Iggy   It's not very interesting.

Tony   What is it?

Iggy   Old-Time Portraits. Folk come in and dress up in Victorian clobber. Or Wild West. Or 1920s gangsters and have their pictures taken. Sepia wash. There's a new one opening near us and they need a photographer.

Kevin   Oh I've seen them, yeah. Oh, I always wondered what sort of people worked in them places.

Iggy   It'll keep the wolf from the door. Get me through college a bit.

Tony   Kev, would you mind?

Kevin *gets up to go inside.*

Kevin   It was nice meeting you, mate. Good luck with the job.

Iggy   Cheers, mate.

Kevin *exits.*

Tony   Well, I'd be lying if I said I didn't want you to stay. Can you come back later? After he's phoned?

Iggy   You're mashed.

Tony   Phone him from here and give him this number.

Iggy   I ain't got his number. A mate o'mine's sorted it out. I better go really.

Tony   So do I not get to see you again?

Iggy   D'you want to?

Tony   Course I fucking want to, Iggy. Course I fucking do. Does that scare you?

Iggy   I'd love to see you again, Tony. I just don't know that it's right.

Tony   Well, it's not wrong, is it? How is it wrong? Is there something you're not telling me?

Iggy   There's nothing wrong about it, it's just. I dunno. I don't know.

Tony   You don't fancy me.

Iggy   It's not that.

Tony   So you do fancy me?

Iggy   I've got to go.

Tony   Come round tomorrow. Before you go. Come round for your lunch.

Iggy *is crying.*

Tony   Don't cry. There's no need to cry. My cooking's not that bad.

They kiss. For a long time. **Monica** *comes to the French windows filing her nails. She watches them. They stop kissing.*

Iggy   I'll see you tomorrow.

Tony   Great. I'll take the day off work.

Iggy *nods and leaves.* **Tony** *watches him go.* **Monica** *steps out.*

Monica   Hey, you'll never guess what. I've got an audition tomorrow. My really great friend Candice phoned earlier. There's this new musical, and they're having trouble finding really great black actresses who can ice-skate. I said, 'Look no further, Candice.' I love that Candice, you know. She's quite fit actually. Great tits.

Tony   Lovely.

Monica   Oh, look, I'm sorry it didn't work out with little . . . thingy.

Tony   I'm a bit mixed up about all this, you know. This isn't what I'd planned. When I went the pub the other night. I didn't think that. Two days later I'd be. So confused. Nice, isn't he?

Monica   Is he?

Tony   Isn't he?

Monica   Whatever. Yeah, I guess he's kind of . . . sweet.

Tony   Eh?

Monica   Truth?

Tony   Go on.

Monica   I don't trust him.

Kevin *comes out.*

Kevin   Neither do I.

Tony   Why not?

Kevin   I dunno, I just don't.

Tony   You'd say that about whoever I got off with next.

Monica   I mean, what was all that bullshit about having to go to a job interview? I mean, come on! That was just like . . . so invented!

Kevin   Did you think so?

Monica   Believe me. I know when people are improvising. And improvising badly.

Kevin   Maybe he's just trying to let you down gently. He's only a kid.

Tony   Why don't you trust him, Mon? Cos he's a scally?

Monica   No. I'm really into auras and he has got such a disturbing one. It's a colour I've never seen before.

Tony   Oh, shut up.

Monica   Look, don't lose your heart or anything to him, babe. Yeah?

Tony   I'm only having a bit of fun. I. If I'm honest, it doesn't feel right.

Monica   See, I knew it. I'm probably just picking up some of your vibes, you know. Anyway he's going to be out of your life soon enough. That much I do know.

Tony   But every time I look at him, I can't help myself. I want to hate him. Cos he's not Frankie. But I don't.

Kevin   His eyes are too close together.

Tony   His eyes are perfectly positioned thank you!

Kevin   I've met lads like him before. That's all I'm tryina say, mate. And that sort are only after one thing.

Tony   All right, so you can't stick him. I think it's up to me who I see. Don't you? You can't just cling on to the idea that I'll never get over Frankie. Cos I will. I have to.

Monica   Does he know you're positive?

Tony   That's none of his business!

Monica   Er, hello? He's having sex with you?

Tony   Safely. Anyway I've got an inkling he knows. He must have seen the pills in the bathroom. He'll either think I am or Kev is.

Monica   What, you don't talk about shit like that?

Tony   Do we have to talk about everything all the time?

Kevin   What d'you see in him?

Tony   Isn't it obvious?

Kevin   He's cute, yeah, but . . .

Tony   Don't you think I like the danger?

Monica   So you agree he's dangerous? That's a good word for him actually.

Tony   Maybe I'm dangerous. Maybe what I feel for him is dangerous.

Monica   Right.

Tony   Christ, I've only known him since Friday night. And I'm all worked up about him. I took one look at him and said, this guy's trouble. But I don't care. You're right. He's too cute.

Monica   Oh, pass me the sick bag. Cute?! What's cute? Bunny wabbits? Furry little kittens? Yukola, Antonio McBonio. And remember rabbits crap everywhere. And cats, yeah, cats have claws.

She thinks she's been terribly profound. **Tony** *rolls his eyes and goes back inside.*

Blackout.

Scene Two

Monday afternoon.

Tony *sits at the table drinking a glass of wine. A bowl of salad on the table. Two plates. The remnants of a meal.* **Iggy**'s *sports bag on the ground.* **Kevin** *sits on the back step wearing a Blockbuster Video uniform. He is putting on a pair of trainers and a funny voice.*

Kevin   'That's due back Wednesday before eleven o'clock. That's due back Wednesday before eleven o'clock. That's due back Wednesday before eleven o'clock.' That's all I'll say for the rest of the day, you know. I could bring a bottle of wine back tonight. You might be feeling a bit funny.

Tony   Why?

Kevin   Well, he's getting off inn'e? He'll be out of your life for ever. Sort of thing.

Tony   Kevin, why do you have to make it sound so dramatic?

Kevin   Dunno. I'm just thinking of you really. He's taking his time. Is he having a crap?

Tony   I don't know, we didn't go into details, I was still eating.

Kevin   It's just I wanna get in and use the ear things. Last week me boss said I had dirty ear holes. Waxy.

Tony   Well, why don't you ask him how long he's going to be?

Kevin   I don't like to put people on the spot.

The back door goes and **Monica** *comes in, beaming. She is carrying a pair of ice-skates.*

Tony   What are you doing here?

Monica   Antonio? Audition? I don't want to tempt fate, but I really think that job is mine!

Kevin   That's what you said after *Mamma Mia*.

Monica   So?

Kevin   Well, that was months back, and you still haven't heard.

Monica   Yeah, but they still haven't said no!

Kevin   You poor deluded fool.

Kevin *goes indoors.* **Monica** *can't believe* **Kevin***'s cheek.*

Tony   Well, he's kind of got a point. I'm not saying you're deluded. Oh, I'll shut up.

Monica   Do you want me to be stuck in that caff for the rest of my life? My first audition in seven months, and you have to be vile about it. Thanks a lot, Tony. Nice one, buddy!

Tony   How did it go?

Monica   They really liked my voice. They were fucking hooked actually.

She swipes his wine and knocks some back.

And I'm pretty sure the director was a lesbian. Fuck did she enjoy touching me.

She laughs cockily and takes one of his cigarettes.

Tony   What's it about?

Monica   It's really interesting actually. It's about this really fierce girl gang in Nottingham, and they hang out at this ice rink. I said, 'That is so uncanny, Pam, cos I spent the majority of my puberty at the Silver Blade in Basingstoke. It's in fact where I first realised I was a lesbian.' Well, you've gotta flirt. My character's called Trish. And she . . . God this is so exciting . . . she dies at the end! I love dying. And my blood slowly seeps over the ice of the rink. And the other gang members gather round and sing this song called 'The Red Rink'. That's the name of the show. *The Red Rink*.

Tony   What did they say?

Monica   When?

Tony   At the end. Did they say 'When can you start?' or something?

She gets her mobile out.

Monica   They don't come out with it outright, Antonio McBonio. But I bet this little baby's gonna ring any moment. Think I'll call Sheila.

Tony   Sheila?

Monica   My agent.

Tony   I thought she got rid of you.

Monica (*on phone*)   Hi, is that Ming? Ming, it's Monica. Book deal? No Ming, it's Monica Murray. Hi. Murray. I used to be a client of Sheila's. Hi. I'm fine. Just about to do *The Red Rink* I think. So! Fingers crossed! Oh, it's this really 'grrrrreat!' new musical about . . . Sorry? Well, yeah, I rang to speak to Sheila. Oh, right. When will she be out of it? No, I mean the meeting. God, that's a long one. It's just she said. Right. Could you tell her I called? Well, I just thought, what with me going into the show. I just thought she might be interested in . . . Right. Right. Oh, I see. Really? What . . . never? Right. Any specific reason? Sorry? Ming? Ming I think I'm breaking up. (*Hangs up.*) I'm going to have to get a new phone.

Tony   So did you have to sing?

Monica   Aha.

Tony   What did you sing?

Monica   What do I always sing?

She pulls her dress over her face and sings 'Lord Here Comes The Flood', a la Bette Midler. As she sings, **Iggy** *comes out of the French windows. He is taken aback by her singing. He gets a bit upset.*

She drops her dress.

Tony (*to* **Iggy**)   You OK? Come here.

Iggy *sits on his knee.* **Tony** *hugs him.*

Monica   Oh, hi, Iggy.

Iggy   Is that what you sang at Frankie's funeral?

Monica   How did you know?

Iggy   Tony told me.

Tony   Monica's had an audition.

Monica   Apparently Jayne Torvill's read the script and thinks it's really shit hot.

Iggy   Who?

Monica   Jayne Torvill. Torvill and Dean? All those sixes?

Tony   He's too young.

She takes one of **Tony**'s *cigarettes. As she lights up:*

Monica (*showing off*)   I told them about Frankie.

Tony   Why?

Monica   Well, like my character gets stabbed, right, and like just dies there. Blood on the white-cold ice of the rink. And I said, 'You know, something similar happened to a really close friend of mine last year.'

Tony   Frankie wasn't stabbed, Monica.

Monica   But he died. And people gathered round. They were all really sympathetic.

Tony   Sympathetic? One of them went through his pockets!

Monica   No, the musical people. I told them about the pockets. They all looked horrified. I thought Pam was going to cry.

Tony   I'll expect a bouquet this afternoon then, shall I?

Monica (*Nottingham accent*)   Don't be facetious Tony. (*Own voice.*) That's quite good, isn't it? (*Nottingham.*) That's really good. I'm doing a Nottingham accent Tony. What do you think?

Tony   It's wonderful, babe.

Monica   Cheers cock!

Iggy   Is Nottingham in South Africa then?

Tony *pisses himself laughing.*

Monica (*own voice*)   Oh yeah, that's right. Go on, laugh at me.

Tony   Lighten up, for fuck's sake. It was only a joke.

Monica   Nice meeting you, Iggy. Will we be seeing you again? I suppose it's going to be difficult, what with your new job and everything. D'you know what I mean?

Iggy   Oh, you never know. Stranger things have happened.

Monica   What time's your train?

Iggy   Are you trying to get rid of me?

Monica   No! No! No! God, you're so paranoid! Jesus! What am I doing even mixing with you guys? I've gotta get me to Stanmore! Got an A to Z Toe?

Tony   In the bedroom, on the shelf.

She goes inside.

Iggy   She's right. I should be getting off really.

Tony   Get off with me.

Pause.

I never was very good at being serious. It was Frankie's biggest complaint about me.

Iggy   I know.

Tony   It's easier to play court jester. I thought I'd lost my sense of humour. But when I'm with you, right. It comes back, crap though it may be.

Beat.

What d'you mean, you know?

Iggy   It's something I've noticed.

Tony   What is?

Iggy   You'll have a laugh rather than be serious.

Tony   What are you? My fucking psychiatrist?

Iggy   You do it all the time.

Tony   You've only known me five minutes.

Iggy   Well, Frankie didn't like it, did he? You just said.

Tony   Do you have to go back?

Iggy   Well, I can't stay here for ever, can I?

Tony   Why not?

Iggy   Well, what about my job? I'm starting a new job soon.

Tony   Yeah, well, I reckon you made that up.

Iggy   Why would I make that up?

Tony   So you don't have to stay here.

Iggy   Tony, I came away for a long weekend. I didn't expect to meet someone.

Tony   And let's face it. You didn't. Well, no one special, eh?

Iggy I don't understand what you see in me.

Tony Fuck off, Iggy. Gorgeous gay lads don't get to your age without knowing it. And older gay men don't let good times like you pass them by. If they can help it.

Iggy You're not old.

Tony Don't.

Iggy And is that all you see in me?

Tony I could come to Manchester if you want.

Iggy You've got work.

Tony I'll take a week off. I took today off.

Iggy There's things you don't know about me.

Tony There's things you don't know about me.

Iggy If you got to know me. You'd hate me.

Tony Try me.

Iggy I have to go.

Tony I don't want you to. I could lie. Pretend. Say fine. Cool. Whatever. But it's not fine. It's not cool. And I'm sick to fucking death of that word whatever.

Iggy I'm sorry.

Tony These things. That if I knew about you I'd hate you. Tell me.

Iggy No.

Tony You think I'd never forgive you?

Iggy No.

Tony I will. I promise.

Iggy No.

Tony If I don't forgive you then I give you the right to stab me. How's that?

Pause.

Have you murdered someone? Is that it? Have you?

Iggy   No!

Tony   Well, it can't be all that bad then.

Iggy   I don't need your forgiveness.

Tony   Do you not?

Pause.

Iggy   Bye, Tony. I'll phone you.

Tony   Fine. Cool. Whatever.

Iggy *kisses him and then heads to the back gate.*

Iggy   The chicken was nice.

Tony   Very tender. The flowers were nice too.

Iggy *looks back.*

Tony   The red roses.

Iggy   Which red roses?

Tony   The ones you put on Frankie's grave.

Pause.

Iggy   Did you see me?

Tony   I didn't need to.

Iggy   How did you know?

Tony   About the flowers? Well, you were fucking him, weren't you?

Iggy   He told you?

Tony   No, he didn't have the backbone. I thought you had to go.

Iggy   How did you know?

Tony I first saw you on March the first, 1998. Frankie was up in Manchester on business. Checking out some clubs for Trade. He phoned me in the afternoon. I was in a cunty mood and we had a row. Nothing major, but after I put the phone down I started to feel guilty. So I decided to be dead impulsive and get on a train. And go to his hotel. I get there in the . . . the evening. And the bloke on reception says he's gone out for dinner. Did he know where? Yes he'd made the booking. He'd gone to Mash. So I go to Mash. And I climb up the stairs. Oh, I'd forgotten to say I was looking devilishly handsome and carrying a big fuck-off bouquet of flowers. I tell the waiter I'm looking for Mr McAdam. He points out the table. There's a waiter standing at the next table. Frankie's sitting there with his hand outstretched. The waiter moves out to reveal that Frankie is in fact holding someone's hand. Your hand. He never held my hand in public. But he's holding your hand. And I hid behind the flowers. And I walked out, backwards. I went outside and stood where he couldn't see me, but where I could get a good look at you. And you were sat there. And you weren't saying much. So little in fact that I thought, this isn't the first time. In fact, this is worse. This has been going on for some time.

Pause.

Did you love him, Iggy? I don't want to call you Brett. Did you?

Iggy I . . .

Tony Did you love him?

Iggy Yes I did.

Tony And did he love you?

Pause.

Did he love you?

Iggy He said he did. But he never left you.

Tony We're not talking about me. We're talking about you two.

Iggy I'm sorry.

Tony It must have really fucked you off that he was with me.

Iggy Maybe.

Tony You didn't have a clue who I was at first, did you?

Iggy *says nothing.*

Tony When I clocked you that night in the pub. I just wanted to be near you. Because you'd been near to him. When did you realise?

Iggy I knew who you were from the off. I'm sorry, Tony. I should be going.

Tony I still don't want you to go.

Iggy I'm not Frankie.

Tony No. But now we've got things out in the open.

Iggy This is too weird. The whole fucking thing's weird.

Tony I know you a little bit now. I know what he saw in you.

Iggy Snap.

Tony Why 'Iggy'?

Iggy Middle name.

Tony I really wanted to hurt you. I really wanted to hate you. And I don't. Thought I'd freak you out bringing you back here that night. And I never.

Iggy Wanna bet?

Tony You're a part of him. You were intimate with him. And I wanted to feel close to him.

Iggy (*shrugs*) Snap.

Tony   And then it all changed. I liked you. And I thought, well, there's no harm in this. We'll have the conversation one day. He'll freak but he'll be fine. And then I think why am I doing this? Am I getting revenge on him? But I don't think I am. I really don't think I am. What did he say I was like?

Iggy   He said you were all right. Said you were good-looking. He showed me a photo. I said I wouldn't kick you out of bed.

Tony   And you didn't. Did he say he loved me? Please feel free to lie, if he said he didn't.

Iggy   I'm not lying. He did.

Tony   Did he tell you I was positive?

Iggy *nods.*

Tony   What did he say?

Iggy   Truth?

Tony   Now feels like as good a time as any.

Iggy   He said he couldn't leave you in case you got ill.

Tony   That tied to me, was he?

Iggy   But he was talking bollocks, want he?

Tony   Was he?

Iggy   Course he coulda left you. If it was that wrong, you and him. And from the sounds of things you've not been that ill.

Tony   Aye, I've been lucky.

Iggy   So he coulda kicked you out at any point. So the way I see it he was just using your . . .

Tony   Status?

Iggy   As an excuse.

Tony   He'd've had a job kicking me out. I bought this place.

Iggy   I used to pretend it fucked me off. I'm sorry, Tony. But I did love him. In my own little way.

Tony   You're not the only one. I knew he shagged around. I've shagged around. But we used to have this agreement. More than once and it's an affair. And that was breaking the rules. No way. But me. I'm a shithouse. A yes man. Didn't even question him. Just thought it would run its course. And nobody else knew. So I was only losing my dignity in your eyes. And you I never knew. He never finished with you, did he?

Iggy *shakes his head.*

Tony   How did you know he'd died?

Iggy   Mary.

Tony   For fuck's sake! Did she know about you?

Iggy   No, don't be soft. I was in his Filofax. Under a false name. She left me a message on me machine. I rang her back and she told me he'd died. Crying me eyes out in the middle of Canal Street. On me mobile. All these queens going past screaming, 'She's been jibbed!'

Tony   Oh you poor wee sod.

Iggy   She said he was struck by lightning in some field.

Tony   It wasn't just any field darling. It was Hampstead Heath. It was mortifying. Burying your bloke when he's died looking for a quick fuck. People laughing at the funeral. Saying what a great fan he was of outdoor pursuits. It's not like it hadn't crossed my mind. I asked Kevin. After he'd died. Whether he'd been having an affair. He seemed really shocked. I was glad. I thought I was Frankie's best mate really. And if he could keep it a secret from me, he could keep it a secret from them.

The doorbell goes. **Tony** *calls into the house.*

Kev? Could you get that?!

They stand there. The doorbell goes again.

Monica?! Sorry, Iggy.

Tony *goes inside. He lets* **Mary** *into the living room. She is carrying a flan dish.*

Mary   I phoned work, but they said you was poorly. I thought, 'He's bunking off.' I bet half o'London's bunking off today. It's glorious. I've carried this all the way on the bus. I made it for me lady with the leg only something happened.

Tony   Mary, this isn't really a good time.

Mary   Oh, all right, darling. I won't stay long.

Tony   You shoulda phoned.

Mary (*to* **Iggy**)   Oh, you're still knocking about, I see. What's your name again?

Iggy   Iggy.

Mary   That's the one.

At the same time as she says this . . .

Tony   Mary. Kev and Monica are inside. Would you mind just . . . I just need a few minutes with Iggy.

Mary   I had an apparition, darling. Hear me out.

Tony   Look, Mary, I'm speaking plain English, will you just get the fuck outta my face?!

Mary   Ooh! Who rattled your cage? You rattled his cage, Iggy?

Tony   I'm sorry but. This is. Oh, what's the fucking point?

Mary   I was just putting the spring onions in this when the face of Frankie appeared to me on me calendar. I've got this calendar with wellknown Jewish people on it. Nothing special, 50p in the jumble. Anyway, this month's Vanessa

Feltz. Only the face of Vanessa Feltz turned into Frankie and he said, 'Give the flan to my old man.' At first I thought he meant his dad. And then I realised.

Tony   Well, take your pick. We're both here. Unless there was someone else as well. Someone we don't know about. It's possible, I suppose.

Mary   I ain't never had an apparition before. You ever had one, darling?

Tony   Mary, Iggy and I are talking.

Mary   About Frankie? Oh, he don't half miss him, Iggy, you know. You can't blame him, babe, you can't blame him. (*To* **Tony**.) Go nice with a baked potato. You've got chives somewhere here. You could bung a few o'them in, babe.

Tony   Iggy misses him too, Mary.

Mary   Do you? Why? Did you know my Frankie? Oh, thank God for that! I thought yous two was getting it on and that. And I don't mean to be horrible, darling, but I thought it was a bit early, you know. I mean he ain't even cold yet, darling. How did you know him, darling?

Iggy   Oh, you know.

Tony   No, she doesn't, Iggy. Why don't you tell her?

Iggy   I knew him from Manchester.

Mary   He went there a few times on business. Doing stuff for Trade. They done a few nights up there and they liked Frankie to go up and case the joints, you know. He was very well respected in clubland.

Tony   He went there a lot on business. And managed to combine it with pleasure.

Mary   Oh, we all like a bit of pleasure, darling. Don't deny him a good time.

Tony   And he was the good time that was had by all.

Iggy   Fuck off.

Mary   No need for swearing darling. Is there, Tony? Tell him, Tony. (*To* **Iggy**.) I don't like your tone.

Tony   Iggy and Frankie were . . .

Iggy   I should go.

Tony   Don't you dare leave me now!

Mary   Where are those chives, darling?

Tony   Frankie was having an affair, Mary. Your flawless perfect son was having it away with Iggy.

Mary   No. No.

Mary *is kneeling down at the chives. She gets a pair of scissors out of her handbag and starts cutting some up.*

Tony   Tell her. She won't believe me. But then you've never believed anything I've said, have you, Mary?

Mary   Eh?

Iggy   It was nothing special.

Mary   Fucking load o'rubbish.

Tony   It wasn't that special? How fucking dare you say that?!

Mary *stands up with a bundle of chives. She hands them to* **Tony**.

Mary   There you go. Is that right, Iggy? Was you seeing my Frankie an'all?

Iggy   Casual.

Mary   Nice lad, darling, wann'e?

Tony   Fucking lovely! The best guy in the land!

Mary   I don't think Tony's very happy about it.

Iggy (*leaving*)   See you.

Mary *grabs hold of him.*

Mary   I don't think you're going nowhere, darling. Give the bloke some respect if you were . . . having it away with his old man. The love of his fucking life, darling. Now I'm gonna let go of you and you're gonna stay. You got that?

Iggy *wrestles with her.*

Mary   Do I have to spell it out to you?

Iggy *stands still. She lets go. He stays there.*

Mary   Sit down.

He sits.

Iggy   You're a fucking hard bitch, aren't you? Frankie was right.

Mary   Me? I'm soft as marge, darling.

Tony   It's got to have been serious! Don't you understand? Cos if it wasn't serious with you it wasn't serious with me!

Mary   This really needs to go in the fridge, Tony.

Tony   Well, put it in the fucking fridge then!

He guides **Mary** *and her flan quite forcefully inside.*

Mary   Don't manhandle me, darling!

She is gone.

Iggy   What d'you want me to say? That he was leaving you for me? He weren't. That he slagged you off non-stop? He never. That I was the love of his life and you weren't? That's bollocks! But it weren't just casual. I loved him and he loved me, just not as much as you. But I still loved him. And it broke me fucking heart knowing he'd gone. And I never said goodbye. And I never went the funeral. And I'd never seen his grave. And I never knew his mates. And they never knew me. What else d'you want me to say?

Tony   I'm jealous. He was out having all the fun and I wasn't. I was boring. I wanna stop being boring. I want to be all those things to you too. I want you to think. Yeah,

Frankie was great. But Tony's better. Cos deep down I know. He was a fucking wee shite. A fucking liar. And it's so easy to lie. It's fucking brave to be honest.

Tony *is crying now.* **Kevin** *comes out.*

Kevin   Everything all right? Mary's crying in there. Going on about some calendar.

Tony   Fuck Mary. You were right all along about her, Kevin, she's a fucking waste o' space. Just like her son.

Pause.

Kevin (*to* **Tony**)   What's he said to you? What's he told you?

Iggy   I haven't said a thing!

Kevin   You've fucking told him, you bastard!

Tony   Told me what?

Pause.

Told me what?

Iggy   Tell him, go on.

Kevin   What have you said?

Iggy   I ain't said out, mate. I didn't need to.

Tony   What you talking about?

Iggy   See, you might think you've got good mates, Tony. But they knew all along.

Kevin   I told you to get out. I knew you were trouble, you lying bastard!

Iggy   Oh and you're not? You fucking psycho!

Tony   You knew?

Kevin   Go on, get out! Get out before I knock you out.

Tony   You stay there, Iggy. You knew?

Kevin   Knew what?

Iggy   He knew me the minute he clapped eyes on me. Why d'you think your mates have been so keen to get rid of me?

Tony *sits down.*

Tony   You knew?

Kevin *shrugs.*

Tony   I asked you. I asked you the night of the funeral. You told me not to be so stupid. *You* told *me*. Not to be *stupid*! You of all people!

Kevin   We'd just buried your boyfriend, Tony. He died with his trousers round his ankles and you're asking me 'D'you think he made a habit of this?' Oh yeah, I'm really gonna rub it in then.

Tony   I don't want your pity.

Kevin   I didn't know for sure.

Iggy   Don't lie!

Kevin   Well, I knew he'd seen someone up North. I didn't wanna know. It was Monica that got the details. Every time he mentioned Brett I just told him I weren't interested. I didn't want him messing you about. I told him to finish it.

Tony   Monica?

Kevin (*to* **Iggy**)   Look at all the trouble you've caused!

Tony   Monica knows?

Kevin   Oh, she got all the gory details.

Tony   How long have you known?

Kevin   Don't be angry with me, Tony. Please. I hate meself, Tony. I do. Don't be angry, with me, Tony. It ain't fucking worth being angry over. He was a cunt. You're right. I'm a cunt. You're a cunt. We're all cunts.

Tony   Do you get some sort of perverse satisfaction out of seeing me suffer?

Kevin   No. Course I don't. How can you say that? I love you, Tony.

Tony   Fuck off!

Tony *headbutts* **Kevin**. **Kevin** *falls back. He sits there clutching his head.*

Kevin   I do!

Tony   Why? Because I'm the only person who'll put up with you?

Kevin   No, because you're my mate.

Tony   I don't need mates like you. Mates is about honesty. I can keep any fucking secret I want from a lover. But not from a mate.

Kevin   Well, that's a bizarre type of psychology. Don't hit me!

Tony   Take a look in the mirror darling. That's bizarre fucking headwork. D'you know why I never told you or Monica? Cos I thought you'd be disappointed in him.

Kevin   You knew?

Tony   Course I fucking knew. I'm not stupid.

Kevin   I wanted to tell you. But each day I never made it harder and harder.

Tony   Don't lie to me, Kevin.

Kevin   Frankie said he was going to finish it. Frankie said it wasn't worth hurting you over.

Tony   Save your breath and get Monica.

Kevin   I'm late for work.

Tony   I said go and get her.

Kevin   She'll freak.

Tony   I'm freaking, Kevin, just get her now!

Kevin   Yeah. Yeah. I'm going, I'm going.

Kevin *goes inside.*

Tony   I think maybe you should get out of the way, darling.

Iggy   I don't wanna leave you.

Pause.

Come to Manchester.

Tony   I can't think about that right now. Sorry.

Iggy   I'll be in the pub. Where we met. I'll wait an hour. Then I'll get off. I know it's fucked up. But I like you. Let's live dangerously.

Iggy *picks up his bag and goes.* **Monica** *comes to the door, shitting herself. She has an* A to Z *in her hands and her bag.*

Monica   Listen, I'm going to have to make this really quick. Do you know how far Stanmore is?

Tony   I know you were Frankie's friend.

Monica   Listen, Antonio Mc . . .

Tony   Don't call me that. I don't like it. I've never liked it. But, 'Oh no,' said Frankie. 'She thinks the world of you. Give her a go.' And you? You used to spout all that bullshit about how good pals we were. Bollocks. I've been made a cunt of.

Monica   I don't like that word. Much.

Tony   I don't like you much. And d'you know why? Cos you're a fraud. Frankie thought you were some sort of intellectual, who made him look clever. But Germaine Greer doesn't work in a caff, does she?

Monica   We've all got to start somewhere! And if anyone's a cunt round here it's Brett. Where is he?

Tony   D'you know why you've never heard from *Mamma Mia*, Monica? Because you probably did their heads in. Like you probably did their heads in today. 'Oh, I'm a lesbian, right.' Like it's going to impress them. Well, go and fucking lick someone out and stop pretending you're my friend.

Monica   That's pretty offensive, Tony.

Tony   I don't give a fuck, you fat talentless bitch.

Monica   I'm outta here.

Monica *goes out.* **Kevin** *comes to the door.*

Kevin   Tony.

Monica *marches back in again.*

Monica   Hang on a mo. Talentless? Talentless? You make it up as you go along, you do. If I was (*Mimes inverted commas.*) 'talentless', why did you ask me to sing at the funeral? That priest was in tears!

Tony   He was probably shagging Frankie as well then.

Kevin   You're being silly now.

Monica (*chuckles*)   A psychiatrist would have a field day with you.

Tony   Ah, but I don't see a psychiatrist, darling, you do. I'm pretty much together, thanks.

Monica   Well, I think it's pretty rich actually.

Tony   What's pretty rich?

Monica   That you're so angry with us. When you should really be angry with Frankie.

Tony   Oh, don't pass the buck, Monica.

Kevin   Well, it's not us that had the fucking affair. I didn't jump on Brett the first time I seen him.

Tony Don't call him that.

Kevin Why not? It's his name!

Monica Because if you call him that it's proof of what a hypocrite you are! You've met him, you like him, you've stuck your cock in his mouth and liked it, and you feel guilty. You feel bad. And so you're taking it out on us. Fine, babe. Whatever. Where is he?

Tony If you weren't a woman . . .

Monica I always knew you were a misogynist.

Tony Oh, don't make me laugh. I don't hate all women. I just hate you.

Monica Displacement!

Tony OK, I hated Frankie. Hated him not telling me. And I was jealous. But see I've had years to work through that one. And ever since Frankie died, all you've done is done my head in. I never told you about Frankie cos I was trying to protect him. And you. Christ knows why!

Monica I'll tell you what you hate, Tony. You hate the fact that you fancy your boyfriend's bit of trade. That's all. And hey, it's no big deal. You'll get over it. I have. You're gay. Be gay. Live up to the stereotype, babe! Have no scruples! Doesn't bother me!

Tony I can't bear to fucking look at you two. No wonder you were both being so vile about Iggy yesterday. Got a weird aura, has he? Eyes too close together? You were just bloody well protecting yourselves. Encouraging me to get rid of him to ease your guilty consciences.

Monica Whatever!

She sits down and consults her A to Z. **Kevin** *edges round and sits next to* **Tony** *and tries the softly-softly approach.*

Kevin Don't be pissed off with me, Tony, please. I never made Frankie have an affair.

Tony *pushes him away.*

Tony   You fucking stink! You always fucking stink!

Kevin *gets up, angrily.*

Kevin   I never made him go on and on and on about how fit Brett was. About all the funny quirky little things Brett said. About how much better in bed he was than you. How his stomach was tighter. How his . . . I didn't say all those things, Frankie did!

Monica (*looking up from her book*)   Yeah and what sort of friends would we have been if we'd repeated that to you?

Kevin   You're just embarrassed cos we know your little secret now.

Pause. **Tony** *sits there and starts to laugh.*

Tony   I must have really fucked you all off, staying alive so long. I really thought you were genuinely happy for me, each time I came back from the clinic. How are the T-cells, Tony? Getting higher and higher. How's your viral load, petal? Getting lower and lower. My HIV's almost undetectable now. Oh fab. And really, your hearts must have been sinking.

Kevin   Bollocks.

Monica   God, you're so self-obsessed!

Tony   Well, I'm so sorry to have disappointed yous.

Monica   Me me me me me! God, you do my fucking brain in, guy!

Kevin   Why did you carry on seeing him when you knew full well who he was? And you reckon I'm fucked up?

Tony   I don't have to answer to anybody here. I'm not in the wrong.

Kevin   No, Tony. You never are.

Monica   Listen, can we continue this another time? I'm supposed to be in Stanmore. Colin and Vince beckon!

Tony   Actually, no, let's not continue this another time. In fact, let's never continue anything ever again.

Monica   Sorry?

Tony   And one way you can do that, Monica, is by never darkening my garden again.

Monica   Oh don't be such a drama queen. I'll give you a call tomorrow. You'll be so over this by then.

She leans in and pecks him on the forehead. He pushes her away.

Tony   You're so thick-skinned, aren't you? Nothing ever really affects you, does it?

Monica   I'm incredibly sensitive actually. It's one of my most endearing qualities. As you'd know if you ever bothered to find out. (*Winks and clicks her teeth at* **Kevin**.) Wish me luck!

She leaves. **Kevin** *stands there.* **Tony** *looks at him.*

Kevin   Do you think I'm in love with you? Do you think I'm that sad?

Tony   Why should I think that?

Kevin   Cos I'm not.

Tony   And the point of this is . . . ?

Kevin   Everyone thinks I am.

Tony   I wish you were.

Kevin   What? Why?

Tony   Maybe you'd have told me sooner.

Kevin   I wish I fucking was. Then it would have made this simple. I wouldn't have been torn like I was.

Tony   I don't really care, Kevin. So save your breath.

Kevin   I'm late for work.

Tony   I think maybe you should investigate finding somewhere else to live.

Kevin   Maybe if I did love someone I'd have a reason to stop drinking.

Tony   Don't do that on my account. It's the only thing that makes you interesting.

Kevin   I don't want to move out.

Tony   We all have to do things we don't like, Kevin.

Kevin   You don't. You have your cake and eat it, you.

Tony   Is that how you see me, Kevin? Mr Hedonism? Who gives a fuck what I do, or who I hurt as long as I'm OK? That's not me. I think of the repercussions.

Kevin   Then think of the repercussions of being with Brett.

Tony   That's nothing compared to the thought of being stuck with you and Monica for the rest of my life. At least I get something out of it.

Kevin   We'll talk later. I could get a video out. A bottle o'wine. I could get a gram of coke. We can talk. Or we'll skip the wine. And the charlie. We can make this right, Tony. I know we can.

Tony   I don't want to.

Kevin   Don't say that.

Tony   Why not? It's the truth. And the truth hurts. Me and you. But I've got to be honest. I do not want to sit in having some girlie chat with you like Ally McfuckingBeal, chewing over the events of the last few years. I'm hurt, Kevin. I thought you were late for work.

Kevin   I'll see you later.

Tony   Don't count on it.

Kevin *leaves.* **Tony** *sits there. He looks at his watch. He gives a big sigh.* **Mary** *appears at the French windows. She holds a spliff in one hand and a plate of flan and salad in the other.*

Mary   You still angry with me? I dunno what it is you think I've done.

He doesn't respond.

You ain't gonna shout at me again, are you?

He shakes his head. She comes out.

Mary   Frankie used to shout a lot. I think I might have frustrated him. You feeling peckish? I cut you up a bit of flan.

Tony   I've only just eaten.

Mary   What did you have?

She puts it on the table. She sits with him and lights up her spliff.

Tony   Roast chicken.

Mary   Nice and moist?

Tony *chuckles.*

Mary   Nothing worse than a dry bit o'chicken. That was one thing I never had to worry about with Frankie. I knew you was feeding him properly. It's different when you're on your own, innit? You don't wanna make the effort. I always feel like I'm in a movie when I sit out here. You know, one o'them pictures where they're all in Italy. And they play tennis. Write letters home. In the twenties, or Edwardian. No it's lovely. She's always in them, thingy. Short hair and big skirts. Emma whatsit, used to be married to ginger Irish bloke with no lips. Had a baby on the Internet.

Pause.

Mary   Where's little Iggy then?

Tony *shrugs.*

Mary Ah, has he done the dirty on you?

Tony No.

Mary Oh. Oh good. Nice-looking lad. Pleasant with it. There's a lot to be said for manners. Ah. My Frankie had good taste in men, didn't he, eh? I always said it. That bloke he was with before you. He was nice an'all. Gary.

Tony Gary's inside for GBH, Mary.

Mary He was provoked though Tony.

Tony Cut the crap, Mary, eh?

Mary I'm only saying how my Frankie had good taste in men.

Tony *smiles.*

Mary I dunno why. He was no oil painting.

Tony *laughs. She laughs too.*

Mary Face like a bulldog chewing a wasp.

They laugh.

Oh, I shouldn't be cruel. His old girl can't have been no oil painting neither eh?

Tony Oh, she's all right.

Mary D'you want some o'this? Oh, go on, I hate smoking it on me own.

Tony I didn't think you had any.

Mary It's yours darling. Hope you don't mind. I was hoping Kev woulda seen Dodgy Rog, but what with it being so hot he'd taken his kids up Victoria Park. Well, you can't blame him. Where is everyone?

Tony Kev's gone to work. Mon's gone to Stanmore. Iggy's gone the pub. I'm going out of my mind.

Mary   It's a busy life, innit? I often envy that Kevin. That's a lovely job, innit? Seeing all them pictures. I wouldn't mind a job like that. He don't drink at work, does he?

Tony   Iggy's waiting for me down the pub. Wants me to go up North with him.

Mary   There's a lot of crime up there. Guns. When my nice lady with the leg went up Manchester to see Daniel O'Donnell she had her handbag slashed. Someone come at her with a pair o'scissors. All she had left were the straps. And her in a wheelchair. There's something wrong there, int there, Tony? Int there though?

Tony   I'm surprised the smell of her didn't frighten them off.

Mary   Well, it's a tough place Manchester.

Pause.

Still. Frankie liked it.

Tony   I've just been quite vile to Monica and Kevin.

Mary   Oh well. Sometimes you can't do right for doing wrong. I feel like that sometimes.

Tony   I don't know whether I was just waiting for an excuse to jib them.

Mary   Ah, they're nice people, Tony. You're all nice people.

Tony   I feel like I've shed a skin. I feel about three stone lighter. (*Suddenly hearing what she said.*) I'm not a nice person.

Mary   Oh, don't say that, you're one in a million, darling.

Tony   I'm boring. I go to work. I sell expensive clothes to richer people than me. I come home. I potter in my garden. Have the odd drink. Take the odd tablet. See the same old boring people, day in, day out. I am, I'm boring.

Mary You wanna be grateful you've got that job. It's a swanky shop, Harvey Nicks. Frankie bought me that makeover there.

Tony He never. I did. He'd completely forgot it was your birthday.

Mary I had a glass o'champagne in the bar. The girl who done me nails said my cuticles were amazing. I know what she meant to say. They were amazing for a woman like me. From my background. Cheeky cow.

Tony Iggy makes me feel exciting again.

Mary I said, 'Don't judge a book by its cover, darling. I was very nearly an opera singer.' But like Frankie said. It's a shop for posh people. That's probably why you feel a bit funny, darling. Why you're snapping and that. Working all day surrounded by snobs. Ain't good for your psyche. Bound to get you down sooner or later.

Tony It's time to move on, Mary.

Mary You should get a job at Marks. That's a lovely shop. Their staff are always immaculate. If you worked up the Angel, you wouldn't have to get up 'til about half eight. Imagine that. Half eight! Life o'bleedin' Riley.

Pause.

Tony It's time to move on.

Mary You're lucky. You can. You can get another boyfriend. I can't get another son.

Tony I've gotta sell this flat.

Mary You can't do that, darling. You can move on, I can't. This is all I've got left of him. No one thought he'd leave it to you. I don't mean to be rude, darling, but we all know you're on your way out. Don't make sense, darling.

Tony Did Frankie say he bought this?

Mary It was his name on the mortgage, darling.

Tony   You really don't know anything at all, do you?

Mary   I know I ain't educated, darling. I left school when I was fourteen. That's the way it was in our house. It don't mean we're stupid though.

Tony   This is my flat, Mary, and I'll do with it what I like.

Mary   You don't wanna sell it when you've got it looking so lovely, darling. You've got a screw loose.

Tony *gets up and locks the French windows with his house keys. He looks back at her.*

Tony   Why do you come here, Mary?

Mary   To see you.

Tony   You never used to like me.

Mary   I didn't know you.

Tony   You do now?

Mary   Cos I miss him. Ain't nothing wrong with that, is there?

Tony   It's not grief that's keeping you here, Mary. It's guilt. There is a difference.

Pause.

Mary   You had any thoughts about what you're gonna plant out for next year, darling? There's so much stuff on the telly these days about it, you're spoilt for choice really.

He approaches her.

Tony   Come here.

He gives her a hug.

Mary   What you doing?

Tony   Shut up.

He stands back.

Mary   You've got a screw loose.

Tony   Will you make sure you click the latch off when you go out.

Mary   Oh yeah. Blows open otherwise, dunnit.

Tony   I'm going the pub.

He pecks her on the forehead. He takes a last look at the place and then leaves. She calls after him.

Mary   Don't mind if I finish this wine off, do you?

Mary *sits smoking the spliff on her own, lost in thought. There is some wine left over from lunch. She picks up a glass and drinks some. Maria Callas starts to play. 'J'ai Perdu mon Eurydice.' The lights fade.*

Lightning Source UK Ltd.
Milton Keynes UK
22 October 2010

161711UK00005B/14/P